LIFE SKILLS FOR TEENS: BEYOND THE CLASSROOM

A FUN AND INTERACTIVE WORKBOOK TO DISCOVER YOUR PURPOSE, MANAGE ANXIETY, AND NAVIGATE UNCERTAINTY

LARISSA LAWSON

CONTENTS

INTRODUCTION

 *Survival can be summed up in three words—never give up.
That's the heart of it really. Just keep trying.*

— BEAR GRYLLS

*Woohoo, sweet sixteen . . . Just two more years, and I will be out of this house
forever.*

Two decades ago, I couldn't wish for anything but more freedom and
independence. I was sick of everyone telling me how I was wasting
my time over a dead interest of mine and to start building some life
skills. I was rebellious and out to do #mything.

But amidst those late-night parties, identity exploration, and bunking
classes, I was scared. I was scared of what the future held. I wouldn't
call myself the brightest of minds, but I was an above-average student.
I had a knack for conceptual learning and was good with writing and
socializing. I knew my GPA would get me into good colleges. What I
was really scared of was what I would do once I was on my own. How
will I survive? What would the future hold? I could barely fold the

laundry properly. How was I supposed to take care of everything from cooking my own food to cleaning the house?

I felt scared because I wasn't sure if I would make it out there or crawl back into my safe space, aka my parent's house. My dad's several attempts to teach me how to pay bills or open an account in a bank were futile as I couldn't look up from my phone. How could I? The world of the internet was fascinating. You might not be able to relate to it today, but in those days, MSN Messenger was the hottest thing in town. From pings to nudges that would shake the whole screen, instant messaging and texting were all the hype.

But some things were similar too. Even then, adults treated us like idiots. They thought we didn't know about anything. They looked down on us and called us irresponsible and careless when we were just trying to survive. It isn't like we purposely wanted to fail at everything we tried, It wasn't that we didn't have ambitions or knew what we wanted from life. It wasn't like we didn't care about the environment and the future of the planet.

We did. But we never got the appreciation for it.

You guys don't, either. Being a mum of two teenagers myself, I know how conscious and woke you are about the environment. My own children wouldn't allow me to buy anything that isn't biodegradable. It's a nightmare going shopping with them.

The point is, I know of the challenges you face. I know that the system has failed you, and you have no one to look up to. You want to grow, explore, and follow your dreams, but you feel stuck because of the lack of available resources.

The world is crueler than ever. Everyone has a point to make. People get offended over the smallest things. They make everything about themselves.

Survival, my child, in this chaotic world isn't simple.

Like some of you, I had to grow up earlier than I should have. My house wasn't the most ideal place. Ambition and passion weren't appreciated. Having an opinion about something equaled misbehavior. Decisions were made for me without my input or consultation. So I know perfectly well what freedom means to you. I know how desperately you want to get away from the chaos and start a life of your own.

But let me tell you this: It won't be easy. I wish the schools were more interested and concerned about teaching life skills than they are about teaching biology or math. No one, literally no one uses the Pythagoras theorem that they made us learn in school back then. I would have appreciated it if they had taught me how to cook, clean, and become financially independent. I would have appreciated it if they had taught me about money-making ventures and savings.

But school failed us. And it still does. It doesn't prepare you for what's to come. And now, the expectations are rising. People are looking at you, left, right, and center. Life is getting messier by the day, and you just want to get by without creating a fuss.

So, my lovely teenagers, it's time to take back control. It's time to let everyone know what you are capable of. You don't need your parent's money or help. You just need the right tools to get through each day, one at a time.

Challenges will keep coming, one after the other. But when you know your basics well, the rest will come easy. Let's figure out things together as a team. Let's do it without any pressure or anxiety.

Let's fill some critical gaps in functionality, self-management, and life skills so that you can learn to fend for yourself successfully in life, which will last a lifetime. It's time to learn who you are and what you want to be. Let's find role models to look up to. Let's gain some much-deserved respect.

It's time you stop trying to fit in and create some room for yourself.

This book will help and direct you. Each chapter comes packed with exercises that I want you to spend a good amount of time navigating and working on. Each chapter holds several questions as well as the answers to them. You just have to be aware enough to find them. Relax—it's possible! I have tried to make it as user-friendly and relatable as possible to guide you on this journey into adulthood without the help of others.

You don't have to do things all by yourself. Let me be your guardian angel. Let me be your fairy godmother and hold your hand along the ride.

About Me

I am an educator and the author of *Life Skills for Teens Beyond the Classroom: A Fun and Interactive Workbook to Discover Your Purpose, Manage Anxiety, and Navigate Uncertainty.*

My work is dedicated to empowering young people to move through life with independence and confidence. My writing is fun and easy to read and aims to provide teens and young adults with guidance they can turn to as they face new challenges in their everyday lives.

Due to my family circumstances when I was younger, I was forced to grow up quickly and learn a lot of the skills I would later need as an adult independently. Now, with teenage children of my own, I have an eagle eye for recognizing the challenges young people face and the skills they need to help them through.

Driven by my own difficulties and struggles as a child and an awareness that the world is rapidly changing, I am committed to helping young people navigate the challenges the education system doesn't equip them for. I volunteer in schools and youth centers, running workshops that aim to give young people the skills they need to grow into independent adults. I am always guided by the groups I work with and aim to make every session fun in a way that works for the dynamic of the group.

I am a Swiss-American and live with my family in California. I love reading, cooking, and discovering new things—which I find my children to be excellent instigators of.

HOW TO ACTUALLY USE THIS BOOK (SO IT DOESN'T SUCK!)

Let's be real. Being a teen is tough. School's stressful. Friends are drama. Parents just don't get it. And on top of all that, you're supposed to be figuring out who you are and what you want to do with your life. *No pressure, right?*

So, you've got this book. Maybe you wanted it, maybe you didn't. Either way, you're probably expecting the same sort of thing you'd find in a cliché self-help book for teens—you know, the ones that magically pop up on your feed instantly after you utter the word "stressed".

This isn't a cliché self-help book for teens.

This book isn't going to lecture you or tell you how to be someone you're not. Working on yourself doesn't mean fitting into a mold. It will help you discover who you are, what makes you tick, and how to make your way through this crazy thing called life, *in your own way.*

Okay, so how do we actually do this? Well, it's not like you can just snap your fingers and suddenly know everything about yourself. It takes work. But don't worry, it's not all boring lectures and stuff.

Each chapter has activities and challenges to help you figure things out. Plus, there are worksheets and prompts to get your brain going.

You're probably thinking: "How will I remember all this?!"

Okay, so maybe you're not the best at memorizing stuff. No biggie. We've got chapter recaps, so you can always go back and refresh your memory. And those worksheets? They'll put everything you're learning into practice, so it becomes second nature. Plus, they're a chance to have some fun and get creative while you're figuring things out.

If you're wondering when it's reading or writing time, this will be obvious. Keep an eye out for the pen and pin symbols—they're your clues on what to do next...

This pencil means it's time to get stuck in. These are exercises you can tackle right away, either in the book itself or using the worksheets at the back. They're like mini-challenges to test out what you're learning. Trust me, the more you do, the more you'll get it.

The pins are more like thought-provoking prompts. No right or wrong answers here, just a chance to let your mind wander and explore different ideas. Jot down your thoughts in a journal, talk them over with a friend, or just let them simmer in your brain for a while. You might be surprised where they lead you!

Ready, set, grow!

So, if you're looking for ways to navigate the ups and downs, the highs and lows, the awkward moments, and the epic wins in teenage life— this book is meant for you. It's packed with practical tips, real-life challenges, and thought-provoking questions to help you:

- Conquer stress and anxiety like a boss, so you can actually enjoy life.
- Build rock-solid friendships that lift you up, not drag you down.
- Deal with family drama without losing your mind.
- Discover your passions and start building a future that excites you.
- Develop the confidence to be unapologetically you.

No more feeling like you're just going through the motions. Get started today to take control, make positive changes, and create a life you love.

You've got this!

Larissa Lawson

I Get It... You're Already Worried About Getting Bored... Am I right?

Kill the boredom and **embrace the journey** with these printable worksheets!

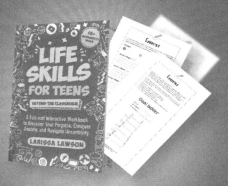

Filled with **interactive activities**, **journal prompts**, and **thought-provoking questions**, these worksheets are designed to spark **self-reflection** and give you space to apply what you're learning.

Scan QR code

(Or visit: larissalawson.com/worksheets)

1

WHO AM I AND WHO I WANT TO BE

 I think every person has their own identity and beauty. Everyone being different is what is really beautiful. If we were all the same, it would be boring.

— TILA TEQUILA

Do you know why we are called the human race? It's because we are always running . . . running after something: a person, career, or success. Throughout the centuries, we have tried to be the next best thing. We want to acquire everything we can get our hands on. A new phone, a new app, a new filter . . . we have tasted it all, and still, the hunger never ends. We want more and more, day after day, to fill an insatiable void we know we can never fill.

Have you ever wondered why we are doing this?

We do this to discover *who we are* and *what we value.*

It is not fame that we are after. We don't want to be soccer players, cheerleaders, or valedictorians. We want to know what interests intrigue us. We want to know who we are. We want to find someone relatable. We crave relevancy. We want to fit in even when we don't know what it means.

Teen years are the years of self-discovery. It's a quest for who you are. It's about finding a purpose to look forward to. It's about wanting to stay relevant. It is both exciting and scary.

Self-awareness, my lovelies, is a beautiful thing, the best of the best. Mark Twain once said, "The two most important days in your life are the day you are born, and the day you find out why" (Mark Twain Quotes, n.d.).

Isn't that what we are all after? To know who we are and what we represent? To know what we want from life, what goals and ambitions we have, what boundaries we establish, and what things we prioritize?

You are not just a pretty face or a nerd behind glasses. Your appearance doesn't determine your character or the values you hold. Your sense of identity has more to do with the way you look, dress, or talk. You are much more than what others believe you to be.

You are a powerhouse, a firecracker, ready to light up and paint the sky.

Your self-concept defines your place in the world. It is important to know where you belong so that you feel safe and happy.

You see, your name was given to you by your parents. The way you look has to do with your genes. Your eye color, hair, and physique are all a combination of your heritage. Your family's socioeconomic status determines the kind of experiences you have. The chances you had or didn't have as a baby were directly proportional to how wealthy or poor your parents were.

But who you are and who you will be is something that only you get to have a say in. That's a personal choice and an important one. Your identity is yours to choose. PERIOD.

But no matter how much you want to feel in control, there will always be people around you giving you unsolicited advice and feedback. Your actions and opinions will never match theirs. You will be compared with someone superior to you. You will forever need to prove your worth to these people. Sometimes, the voices will get so loud that you will have a hard time hearing what your heart and mind tell you. The noise will hit through the roof and deafen your ears along with your ambitions and will.

If only you had the powers of Eleven from *Stranger Things* to wreak havoc and telekinetically push everyone aside.

The worst happens when we keep listening to what others say about us and then, one day, start believing it too. It isn't uncommon that when people tell you something repeatedly, over and over again, you start believing it to be true. Maybe I am not cut out for this sport as my father tells me. Maybe I don't have what it takes to be an actor. Maybe I should just quit trying my luck and do as my parents tell me to do.

That's when you give away your power. You hand over control of your life to others. You give them a chance to manipulate and hurt you.

And don't forget that even then—after complying with whatever your parents and society tell you—you will be called labels. Oh, you don't know what to pick as your major in school? How indecisive of you. Oh, you need more time to finish up an assignment? You are a procrastinator. Oh, you want to do something else other than sports? What a quitter you are!

Don't let these labels become who you are. Don't prove them right. You have a choice. You have tough decisions to make. You have to call the shots yourself. If you don't do that, someone else will—on your behalf.

Who you choose to be today will lead to the choices you make, the actions you take, and the results you yield.

This choice is your identity. Your identity is what makes you stand out from the crowd. It's the difference between you and me. You are you, and I am me. We aren't the same. We might look similar, but our aspirations are different and unique. We have different values and perspectives to view life. We aren't cut from the same cloth.

How you see yourself is important because it is what drives you, sets your attitude, and influences your behavior. Self-perception also affects how you feel about yourself, what value you hold, and your worth. A strong sense of self makes a big difference. According to a licensed counselor, Erika Myers, "Having a well-developed sense of self is hugely beneficial in helping us make choices in life. From something as small as favorite foods to larger concerns like personal values, knowing what comes from our own self versus what comes from others allows us to live authentically" (Hodges, n.d.). This means if you think poorly of yourself, your choices and behaviors will show a lack of self-worth in everything you do. If you think poorly of yourself, you will never have the will to go after the big things because you will think you don't deserve them.

Your self-perception fuels recognition of your own worth. It determines what value you have in the eyes of others. With self-awareness, you can know your goals and purpose. You can be aware of your strengths and weaknesses. You can address areas of improvement to make the most of your God-gifted abilities and talents.

In short, you don't have to live by any stereotypes or preconceptions. You don't have to abide by the social norms set by others. You can choose your own path, your identity, and your passions.

You may say, "Hey Larissa, cool, but what if I don't have any idea who I am?"

No worries. Just keep ~~swimming~~ . . . I mean reading (channeled my inner Dory for a moment).

First things first, don't freak out. Discovering who you are, or are supposed to be, is part of growing up. According to a 2015 study, 37%

of young adults struggle with their identities (Schwartz et al., 2015). Besides, you don't have to figure everything out all at once. Your hormones are at play and might deceive you into thinking you are someone else. Therefore, give it time.

Also, since the teen years are the age of exploration, new bonds, and experiences, there is a chance you might be different around certain people. Your attitude might differ in different companies. You might be a social butterfly among your friends but not so social and open with your family. Similarly, you may act all disciplined and organized at school, but your parents can't say the same about you after looking at your room. The point is that you can be a lot of things, so keep discovering yourself and gaining self-awareness through different experiences.

You may also be experimenting with your moods and attitudes to know where you fit in. For example, you might dress a certain way to be accepted by a certain crowd, choose activities that only specific people opt for, or form relationships with like-minded people just to feel secure.

Lastly, your own culture and external environment will influence your identity too. The values your family has upheld throughout your infancy have roots within you. The language you speak, the way you dress, and how you interact with people impact the way you view your identity.

So if all these factors affect the way you think, approach, and view things, you must learn who you want to be based on what you already know about yourself.

WHO AM I?

Let's start with the very basics. What are acceptable and unacceptable behaviors according to you? What boundaries do you have? What values will you never compromise on? What are your passions and goals you want to pursue in life? What gives you a sense of purpose and excitement? What activities make you feel good and positive about your life?

Alright, maybe I came on a bit too hard with the questions. Let's think about each one individually and see where it all leads to. Let's begin with the establishment of healthy boundaries.

Healthy boundaries are like an invisible fence that keeps out everything that isn't acceptable. This includes people, thoughts, and opinions. Know what you are comfortable with.

A healthy boundary is what limits the entry of anything unwanted in your life, be it in the form of a joke, insult, or individual. You decide the way you want to be treated without any shame or guilt. Doesn't that make you feel powerful already? You can choose to spend time with whomever you want, give your mental health some peace, and free yourself from unsolicited emotions. This way, you can remain solid, content, and resilient. A protective barrier prevents you from being drained, manipulated, or used. Healthy boundaries, although not always clear, let others know what you will and will not tolerate. You can take charge of your life with good personal boundaries and lead a well-balanced life. You can devote the time and energy to try figuring out your passions and invest in them wholly.

Without these boundaries, you will remain tangled up in familial obligations, expectations, relationships, and work and lose yourself in it. You will be exploited and taken advantage of by those who themselves have no filters or boundaries.

Establish healthy boundaries and say yes to the things you want to say yes to. Use healthy boundaries as an internal compass to guide you. Do what you love and say no to anything that doesn't serve you.

Another insightful way to know who you are is to know your values and beliefs. What values and traits do you hold dear? What are no-no characteristics, according to you? What behaviors will you never tolerate?

Personal values are things important to us—things like family, friends, good health, security, loyalty, freedom, and so on. Our values set the theme of everything we do. Like Billie Eilish's number, it is what helps us make sense of things. Our values are always there, a product of our subconscious, paving the way for our thoughts, actions, and desires. It is your values and your family's that have brought you where you are today. What you find acceptable might not be acceptable to someone else. What qualities you look for in someone are also because of the values you hold. If you value honesty and trust, you look for that in everyone you meet. If you value good looks and status, then that is what guides your actions and interactions.

Values can also be your goals. What you aspire to be may be motivated by a value. For example, if you value traits like helpfulness, you might enter professions like medicine, law, or hospitality.

The values you have were given to you by your parents. Some of them were modeled by the company you kept or the people you interacted with in your community. This means that values aren't always perpetual. They can change over time, given the circumstance you are in. If you move to another country or start hanging out with a different crowd, your values might change. You may adopt the ones they have and forget your old ones.

During adolescence, young adults like you may rebel against the old notions they had. Through experiences and insightful situations, their perception might change. You may find a bigger purpose to work for, changing all that you believe in. For example, a traumatizing incident or heartbreak may alter your outlook toward life.

Since your identity is linked to the values you treasure, think logically about the ones you have. Are they motivating you to do better in life or holding you back from pursuing your goals? Keep learning and exploring. Your values will determine your actions. Good values like time management, honesty, kindness, empathy, and so on will cultivate a sense of satisfaction, contentment, and inner stability in life.

Knowing about your passions and interests can also tell who you are. Picture this: You took a summer job at an elderly home just to fill in for your sister, who bailed out at the last minute. You had made plans to go where all your friends were interning but alas. Every day becomes a struggle. You dread going to the elderly home every day because there isn't anything to motivate you. The job specifications are dull. The tasks are repetitive and nothing super exciting. It's a gloomy place to be in, knowing that all your friends are having the time of their lives at their summer job at the fancy hotel by the beach.

You feel stuck and unhappy. You know you aren't doing what you should be doing. Now imagine if you could get out, leave that job, and join your friends at the fancy hotel. You always wanted to get into the hospitality industry, and this is the perfect opportunity to try your luck. You wake up feeling excited about the work as well as meeting your friends. There is excitement and happiness. Every day is a new day just waiting to happen. The work doesn't put you off. The hours just go by.

Your passions work the same. If you don't pursue something you love, you will feel like life is a burden, a struggle. You will find it unfair and tedious. On the other hand, if you follow your passions, go after your goals, and have a purpose to work toward, that's where all the excitement lies. Passion adds motivation and excitement to life. It gives you something to look forward to. It is what leads to a fulfilling life, knowing that you aren't wasting any minute of it.

Your identity has a lot to do with the kind of engagements and interests you have. Passions are driven by the things we enjoy doing. Some find peace and quiet in music, while others are all about making videos and dressing up. Some are motivated by a particular sport, while others are all about entrepreneurship. Whatever gives you the kicks and makes you thrilled is your passion.

Pursuing a passion makes you feel good and energetic. It makes life more meaningful. It shapes and establishes the way you are, the people you connect with, and the actions you take.

Furthermore, know what you want right now. What are your current goals and ambitions? Your identity is also linked to what you want to do with what you have right now. Suppose there is a purpose in your life; what efforts are you making to fulfill it? What steps are you taking to ensure progress and growth? Are you doing enough or barely making things work?

This is something you need to ponder over. Your goals may change ten years from now, but what you want today is significant too. It is what will pave the way for future goals.

Let's learn how to set goals in some fun and interesting ways. Have you heard about the goals ladder?

A goals ladder is an illustrative representation of a goal.

Exercise

On top of the ladder, write a goal that you aspire to achieve. It could be anything as basic as paying more attention in class or as complex as learning a new language. Once you have that ultimate goal in your mind, on each step of the ladder, list one step you will have to take to move higher.

For example, if the goal is to learn to play a new instrument so you can play it for an audience at your school, the first three or four steps might look something like this:

→ Gather the means to buy/rent the instrument.
→ Research YouTube or beginner courses online.
→ Practice for two hours every day.
→ Learn how to play a new tune every day.
→ Play in front of friends and family and gain an audience, and so on.

Goal ladder

My goal: _____

My deadline: _____

My signature: _____

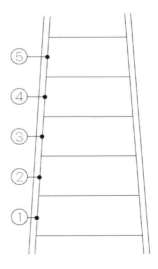

Start higher on the ladder when your
goal has fewer steps!

Another excellent piece of advice comes from Warren Buffet, the world's leading business magnate. He presented his 5/25 rule formula to prioritize the most important goals in life when you have too many (Sidibé, 2022).

Exercise

The idea is simple. You take a piece of paper and write your top twenty-five goals. Then you circle five you consider the most important. Once you have those five out of twenty-five goals, you forget about the remaining twenty and dedicate your focus, conviction, and attention to the five you selected. These are the goals you should solely be focusing on because they mean the most to you.

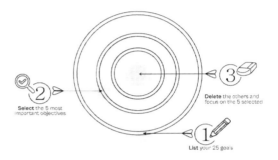

Select the 5 most important objectives

Delete the others and focus on the 5 selected

List your 25 goals

In this way, you can identify the goals that mean the most to you and use the available resources to achieve them. These goals are what your personality and identity are based around. They are what make you who you are. They govern every decision you make in life. They drive your actions. They affect your behavior. They decide who you hang out with, what you do in your free time, and what values you hold close.

If you still continue to battle with these concepts, here are some questions I would like you to answer. These questions and many more like these will help you gain self-awareness and learn about your goals and passions:

- Is there someone you look up to? Who is it, and why?
- What values or traits do you admire or look for in a person?
- What does the word "success" mean to you?
- What activity or person makes you forget all the bad things in your life?
- How would you define freedom and control?
- Are you the same person you were five years ago?
- Do you think you are a good human being? Why or why not?
- If you were asked to describe yourself in three words, what would you say?
- What are your guilty pleasures?
- What's your biggest dream in life?
- What is that one quality you are most proud of in you?
- How would you describe a perfect day?
- What do you wish you had more of in life?
- Are you on good terms with your parents and siblings? Do you think they get you?
- If you could go back in time, what would you change about yourself or your life?

You can also take online personality tests to learn about yourself. While answering the questions, there will be times when you will find out things about yourself that you aren't comfortable with or approve of. Never fear—we all have habits we would like to change about ourselves. I, for instance, would like to become a morning person. I would prefer getting up an hour or two earlier and using that time to do some exercises and mentally prepare myself to go through the day.

You might come across something similar, like your habit of procrastinating, your poor time management, your inability to finish things, or your lack of motivation toward a passion.

Don't get annoyed or demotivated. Don't feel like you have to depend on your parents because you feel incompetent at everything—practice self-acceptance. Appreciate yourself for your flaws. Knowing them is the key to overcoming them. When you have the wisdom and will to change, only then can change happen.

Practicing self-acceptance will also help you feel good about yourself. While you may find something upsetting about yourself, you will also discover all the goodness and wholesomeness in you. Chances are, the positives will outweigh the negatives, and that is what you must celebrate.

Interactive Element

Here's something more interesting and fun to look at. As an adult, I want to help you find the resources that will help you enjoy that freedom you will soon experience. I want you to make the most of it and, for that, you are going to need to start with the basics.

Since we talked about two important things in this chapter, let's see how we can implement that knowledge and put it to use.

The two main themes of this chapter included discovering your core values and setting goals.

Let's begin with values.

Exercise

Here's a list of values every teenager like yourself should manifest and adapt. Check off the ones you think you have. Working on the remaining ones is the real goal. **Prioritize them so that you can focus on one thing at a time and fully understand its essence.** For example, if you think you can do more with some clarity in your life, work toward achieving it. **Make it a priority.** Then, **focus on another value** that you want to nurture and **keep moving.**

- ☐ Advocacy
- ☐ Adventure
- ☐ Affection
- ☐ Ambition
- ☐ Balance
- ☐ Clarity
- ☐ Compassion
- ☐ Connection
- ☐ Communication
- ☐ Courage
- ☐ Creativity
- ☐ Curiosity
- ☐ Dependability
- ☐ Diversity
- ☐ Empathy
- ☐ Forgiveness
- ☐ Freedom
- ☐ Friendship
- ☐ Generosity
- ☐ Gratitude
- ☐ Growth
- ☐ Honesty

- ☐ Humor
- ☐ Inclusivity
- ☐ Inspiration
- ☐ Integrity
- ☐ Intelligence
- ☐ Kindness
- ☐ Leadership
- ☐ Love
- ☐ Loyalty
- ☐ Passion
- ☐ Patience
- ☐ Personal development
- ☐ Power
- ☐ Resilience
- ☐ Respect
- ☐ Security
- ☐ Transparency
- ☐ Wellness
- ☐ Willingness
- ☐ Wisdom

Notice how simple it is to get started?

However, knowing yourself is just the start. It isn't the ultimate goal. The ultimate goal is to learn vital life skills to lead an independent, confident, and fulfilling life. So what's the next step, you ask?

The next important thing you need to do right now is create a goal planner.

Exercise

A planner will help you identify your top goals, list the steps you need to take, and track your progress. Start with a basic goal planner with just one to three goals you wish to achieve per week or month. It should look something like this.

GOALS

1   2   3

Action Steps: Goal 1

_____

_____

_____

_____

Action Steps: Goal 2

_____

_____

_____

_____

Action Steps: Goal 3

_____

_____

_____

_____

Now, let's move on to how to create a personal brand that represents your core values and identity.

CHAPTER SUMMARY

 ## Chapter Summary

Meet yourself. Knowing who you are as an individual and what role you play in this world. **Understanding** what you bring to the table and how **self-perception** shapes your habits, values, and opportunities.

KEY TAKEAWAYS

 ## Key Takeaways

1. The teenage years are the time for **self-discovery** and **exploration**.
2. Choosing who you want to be today leads to more informed and **well-made choices, actions, and habits**.
3. Identify **acceptable/unacceptable values, behaviors, and boundaries**.

SUMMARY

 # Summary

The quest was to help teenagers like yourself to discover their identity. **"Who Am I?"** was a theme we explored and understood.

With the help of some exercises, the goal was to enable youngsters to find what they are capable of and built for. Discussion about healthy boundaries and how it helps shape character and personality were also discussed briefly. Other more important subjects explored included:

→ **A look at the values** you have been brought up with. Sometimes, we need to question some too. These are the ones that hold you back from achieving your goals. It is important to identify them and see how you can create better values instead.

→ **The impact of passions** and interests. They, too, will help you determine who you want to be or what you want in life.

→ **The importance of goal** setting in life. Goals help us achieve our desired lifestyle. They give us a purpose to pursue. They motivate us to keep moving. They build resilience in the face of adversity.

→ Overall, the focus of the first chapter was to help teenagers **seek self-awareness** and use that to fuel their purpose and goals in life. The more they know about themselves, their strengths, and their limitations, the more successful they will be.

2

DEVELOPING A PERSONAL BRAND

 Everyone is comparing lives on social media and wants the perfect body, perfect image, perfect outfit, perfect life—we're striving for this perfection, and it's so unhealthy because there's no such thing as perfection.

— EMILY ATACK

As humans, we have always wanted to have the most power and control. We want to rule the world. We want to make decisions for ourselves. We want to rely on our gut feelings to propagate who we are. We don't want to be in the crowd but the one the crowd is around. In short, we all want to be a brand of our own.

When browsing through channels, I have often wondered what makes some advertisements stand out. Is it humor, innovation, a catchy tagline, or a tune? As a consumer of this bombardment, I have always felt that products and services that are the loudest fail to deliver on the promise and value they talk about. They may have captured our hearts with a cheeky ad about a family moving into a newly painted home, but will the buyer go back if the product fails to deliver? Absolutely not!

The gimmick loses its appeal the minute a product or service fails to deliver.

So just because a brand has a big presence doesn't mean it is the best out there.

The point I am trying to make here is that we aren't always what we put out in the world. Like most big brands, we love the attention and appeal we have. We love getting noticed by the right people who will contribute to our story. But what happens when they don't see what they expected?

Any good, sustainable, and innovative brand relies on its quality. The test is how well the product does after the first buy. Will the consumer come back for it or not? It is quality that makes or breaks a product.

The same is the case with us. When we fail to be who the world thinks we are, we become a failed product. No one wants to be around us after the first interaction.

The image the world has of you is important. It is a direct portrayal of your identity and personality. Think of yourself as a book with a creative book cover. It is both appealing and likable. But what if you are a good book with a hideous, confusing front cover? How many will buy it?

People make assumptions and opinions about you based on what you choose to reveal. This brings us to a more important question: What are you putting out there?

Put down the book and think about it for a minute.

Exercise

Take a sheet of paper and **draw a logo that represents you.** It doesn't have to be a pro's work. **Nobody has to see it.** You can pick an animal, object, or quote... whatever feels comfortable.

Once you are finished with the drawing, take a good look at it, and notice what it signifies. Does it signify the values that you live by? Does it speak of your abilities and talents? Does it portray any skills you have or wish to have?

As important as creating a personal brand is for you, so is putting out the right "YOU." The goal should be to attract like-minded people. It is only possible when they see you for what you represent.

WHY FIRST IMPRESSIONS MATTER

This calls for knowing how to make a good first impression.

Recall the time when you met a teacher or friend for the first time. What was that one thing that stood out about them? What was the first thing you noticed? Was it the way they dressed, their style of walking, their appearance, or the way they talked? Was it a friend who saved you from bullies on your first day of high school, a music teacher that appreciated your understanding of music, or a friend who had an adorable dog?

Now, remember how that one noticeable thing set an impression about them in your mind. How long did it take to change that perception about them (given it wasn't a good one)? As humans, we are hardwired for quick thinking. Did you know that it takes us roughly seven seconds to form a fully-fledged impression about someone (First Impressions, n.d.)?

We make snap decisions about others. We take a second to judge them without knowing where they are coming from. The same applies to you too.

There is substantial research that confirms the importance of good first impressions while exploring several contributing factors. According to a 2009 study, factors such as your clothing style and your posture play a key role in forming the opinions others have about you (Naumann et al., 2009). This means that if you own what you wear and have a confident walk, people will see you as dominant, in control, and wise.

Another study revealed that the way you shake hands with someone can also be a key factor in how people think about you (Bernieri & Petty, 2011). Is it firm and steady or shaky?

People judge you the second you step into a room, from the way you are dressed to how you talk. Therefore, it is vital that you make a bomb-ass first impression whenever you go to a new place or meet new people.

For a teenager like yourself, first impressions mean everything. The right impression helps you attract the right friends, gain acceptance among peers, and connect with your teachers. Whether you are entering middle or high school, it's important to set the right foot forward from day one. First impressions are seen as a segue into social life and what opinions others have of you. It is particularly hard to change once someone has formed an opinion about you.

As a student, you are at an age where everyone will have something to say about you—the way others see you will hold value. A good relationship with your teachers can translate to glowing references and recommendations. A good relationship with your friends can mean a strong support group. Therefore, it is natural to care about how you are seen by others.

FACTORS THAT AFFECT FIRST IMPRESSIONS

Now, there are many things that influence the kind of impression you make. Most of the opinion formation happens on a nonverbal level. You may not be aware of it, but someone might have perceived you in a certain way. The first important factor, therefore, is sensory. How you are dressed, the sound of your voice, or what cologne you are wearing are all ways that play with one's senses and form an impression.

For instance, if you aren't dressed well when you meet someone new or have your hair all messed up, you might come off as lazy and uncivilized.

Second, your posture and the way you carry yourself also say a lot about who you are. Your body language, thus, also becomes a determinant of who you are as a person. Does your voice quiver when you meet someone new? Do you avoid eye contact or have your arms crossed? These are all indicators that you lack confidence.

There is an unspoken norm that most of us, whether we are aware of it or not, prefer people who are similar to ourselves—people who have the same personality, attitude, or beliefs. Following a common belief, religion, or culture also helps set impressions. Stereotyping certain people also affects the way we form opinions about others. For example, just because you belong to a certain religion, you are seen as devoted, respectful, and honest. But stereotyping isn't always accurate. Just because a guy happens to be a popular kid in school doesn't mean he will be a jerk. Just because someone is shy doesn't mean they are an idiot or an outcast.

Another thing that shapes our opinions about others is what they have gone through. Have her parents just separated? She must be vulnerable and depressed. Has he just won a scholarship? He must be over the moon. People's situations and circumstances can also affect how we view them. For example, if you go in for an interview and stumble a little upon entering the room, the interviewer might perceive you as clumsy. But as the interviewee, you might blame poor carpeting or uneven flooring at the company, giving you the impression that they don't care about their employee's welfare.

Exercise

Let's make things a bit more interesting by playing a game. I will give you a few features or behaviors, and you write down your likely first impression about that person. Let me explain it using a few examples.

Observed Feature/Behavior.	Likely First Impression
Smart dressing	Successful
Appearing wealthy	Influential/important
More eye contact	Confident
Speaking faster	
Biting nails or fidgeting	
Driving recklessly	
Sitting alone eating lunch	
Anxiously pacing in the room	
Confident walk	
Gaudy accessories	
Messy hair	
Worn-out shoes	
Shyness	
Manipulative attitude/overconfidence	
A walking talking brand endorser	

GETTING IT RIGHT THE FIRST TIME

Before you misunderstand the importance of a good first impression, know that it has to come from the real you. You might don fashionable clothes, but it is your personality that stands out. If you are trying to please everyone, don't. It's better to be your authentic self than someone you are not. You may fool a couple of people but not all.

However, there are a few basics that you can take care of, given you wish to make a good first impression. This applies to wanting to go for an interview, going on a date, or a social gathering with your friends.

Be Presentable

Always ensure good hygiene. Your clothes should look clean and well ironed. They shouldn't crumple or look stained. Your body should smell nice too. The cologne should be subtle and long-lasting. This doesn't mean you bathe in it before a big date. Your hair should be combed neatly and styled to suit the appropriate event. Your nails should be filed and your hands well moisturized. Your shoes should match the overall outfit and theme you are going for.

Although there isn't anything wrong with wanting to accessorize, take note of the event you are attending and accessorize accordingly. There is nothing wrong with wanting to leave some of the jewelry at home if you're going for an interview or meeting with your supervisor.

Remember, the right outfit doesn't have to be new or fancy. It should look and feel comfortable. It should give you the confidence you need to handle any challenge. It is your confidence people will remember. I know some people who would leave new shoes for a special day and ruin it by feeling uncomfortable all day. Therefore, try on the outfit and shoes a couple of times before the big day (whichever it is).

Be Attentive

I am sure you must have come across some teenagers who believe the whole world revolves around them. They think of themselves as gods. Everything is about them. They are full of themselves and never give another person a chance to share their opinions without being countered. Well, you know the kind of impression you have of them. Certainly, you won't go around wanting people to say the same about you, right? Therefore, whenever you talk to someone, make sure they feel heard. Pay attention to what they are saying, spare their needs some thought, and give them a fair chance to communicate their desires.

Create an Unforgettable Impact

Ever wondered about the kind of impact you have on others? How do they act when you are around? Do they feel at ease, more relaxed, or run the other way? To make a good first impression, ensure that your presence makes people feel warm and positive. It shouldn't scare or frustrate them. Imagine going on a road trip with someone who can't stop talking about themselves, the dark adventures they had, or how challenging it was for them to get their McDonald's order correct from the driveway.

Stay Conscious of Body Language

Our body has a language too. It conveys a message. Whether we are scared, worried, or just plain bored, it gives it all away. Sometimes, it speaks more than your tongue. Therefore, be careful of it. Make your stances, gestures, and body reactions appropriate. For example, when meeting someone new, don't appear all uncertain, forced, or uninterested. Make others feel welcome. They should see you as an approachable and open person. Here are some tips to remember:

- Turn your body toward the person you are speaking to. Angle it in a way that your back doesn't face them.
- Keep your arms to your side and not crossed across your chest. Having crossed arms indicates a closed-off attitude.
- Make consistent eye contact. It suggests intrigue and interest. This doesn't mean you stare into someone's eyes. Just make it seem natural while having a conversation with someone for the first time.
- Avoid fidgeting visibly. Fidgeting indicates boredom. Keep your hands and legs from moving too much. Audibly tapping your foot on the ground can be subdued to slow wiggling.
- Grab a hand when someone reaches out. Hold it firmly and confidently when shaking it. The right grip represents self-confidence and high self-esteem. A weak grip translates to anxiety and insecurity. A good handshake should last two seconds. Anything shorter or longer won't feel appropriate.

Have a **positive** demeanor.

Imagine this: It is your first day of high school. You don't know anyone. At the entrance, you find two teenagers your age. One is Brandon, and the other is Nathan. Brandon sees the best in everyone. Although a newcomer himself, he is optimistic about high school. He knows he might have to face seniors looking out for gullible juniors, yet he knows high school will be the best time of his life.

Nathan, on the other hand, isn't so optimistic. He gets agitated easily. He is cautious, not too welcoming, and somewhat cold. He is someone who wants everything to go as planned. When it doesn't, it upsets him. He is worried he will be a key target of bullies. He has already made up his mind about high school and how it's going to suck.

Now, who would you befriend? The upbeat Brandon or pessimistic Nathan? I bet you answered Brandon. There is just something so positive about him that you would want to hang out with him. This is the aura of positive people. They attract others to themselves. Their casualness and upbeat nature give them a kick-ass attitude. According to one research study, success also depends on how positive you are (Dimberg & Söderkvist, 2011). Did you know that 85% of us succeed because of the mindset we have (Mann, 1918)? Only 15% succeed based purely on their skills or abilities. This proves that your attitude has more to do with how successful you are than your God-gifted skills.

A positive attitude is, therefore, important to create a long-lasting and memorable first impression.

Smile

This brings us to the significance of another important feature: your smile. Smiling is contagious. Try it yourself. Go to a crowded place and pretend to watch something funny on your phone. Then start laughing out loud and see how others around you do the same. They have no clue why you are laughing, but they will laugh too.

Ever looked at a smiling, giggly baby without smiling back? Ever seen someone be unkind to their dog who waited by the door all day for them to come home? Smiling makes you appear more approachable and courteous. It makes you easier to connect with. Did you know, according to some studies, it is almost impossible to frown at someone smiling at you (ScienceBlog.com, 2002)? So why not smile more?

Be Considerate and Kind

I have known some kids around my children's age who want to appear more entitled than others. They want all the attention to themselves. They want to act as if they are superior, more sensible, and wiser than others. This isn't a quality to nurture. It leaves others feeling stupid or like a loser. If you want to make a good first impression, try not to appear better than everyone else. You may be a know-it-all but keep it to yourself. Not everyone appreciates the rudeness and arrogance that comes with it. Be respectful and courteous. This applies to everyone you meet, especially the people who serve you your food or clean up after you. They aren't below you. They are trying to earn honest money. Don't shame them for trying to make a decent life for themselves and their families.

Value Time

Lastly, value others' time. Not everyone has free time to spare. Therefore, if you have committed to meet someone at a designated time, have the courtesy to get there at least ten minutes before that time. This includes all your dinner dates, doctor appointments, interviews, and more. Being punctual shows people that you aren't careless and that you value time.

PERSONAL BRANDING 101

Making a good first impression is important because you want to create a personal brand. A personal brand tells a story about you. It is the story others hear. Your personal brand introduces you in the best light possible. It is what allows you to stand out from the crowd and showcase what you are made of. It focuses on highlighting your skills and unique strengths.

Think of it as a new startup. To ensure it succeeds, you need the right product/service, distribution, and marketing. Its success depends on whether it delivers the promise or not. Personal branding is the same. Instead of a product/service, you create a portfolio of your skills and values.

When you wish to create a strong personal brand, you must appear trustworthy. If it were a business, people would only buy from you if they could rely on your products/services.

With personal branding, you create a strong persona based on your ethos, goals, and missions. Famous people like Oprah Winfrey, Mark

Zuckerberg, and Jeff Bezos all represent a brand. Every time you hear their name, a certain image of them emerges in your mind. You instantly recall what they do, represent, or are famous for. A strong personal brand does the same for you. It allows others to create a mental image of you based on your strongest skills and standout qualities.

Personal branding makes you a marketer. You have to sell yourself in a positive and sophisticated light. You have to gain respect, appreciation, and recognition by showcasing what you are made of.

In today's day and time, when our attention spans have gotten shorter, creating a long-lasting impression is more important than ever. We have become dispensable. Unless we succeed in creating a lasting impact, people will forget about us. They move on to the next big thing and then the next.

The best way to ensure you aren't forgotten is by creating a strong and imperishable brand image. Your brand image should be genuine and accurate as you are going to live and breathe it.

To create an impactful personal brand, find out about your likes and dislikes. Your brand should align with the values and goals you have. It should reflect your interests and likes. Recall all the attributes that make you "you." What is your ultimate goal in life? Do you want to be a professional singer? Market yourself as one. If you want to be a sportsperson, make sure your skills speak for themselves.

Furthermore, have a strong social footprint. Today's the age of social media. Your online presence should reflect your passions and interests as well. That's how you will connect with like-minded people. Go on forums and join groups relevant to your interests. Maximize the knowledge you have by interacting with those more skilled and experienced than you. For example, if you are active on Facebook or Instagram, consistently reach out/follow people who are in the same industry as you. See what they are doing and add those qualities or skills to your personal brand—adopt those habits and behaviors that inspire you the most.

Your brand should also tell a story about you. Where you come from, what values you hold, what traditions you follow, and so on are important aspects of who you are. To build a compelling brand, ensure that the narrative is strong and consistent with your values. How do you plan to cut through the noise? What makes you unique? Does your race, religion, or ethnicity have something to do with your actions?

Your story should be unique. It should make others intrigued. It should get them curious enough to get to know you. Your personal brand should also encompass your struggles, hardships, and experiences. What has led you to become the person you are today? Know that and make sure your story reflects that too.

GETTING TO THE NITTY-GRITTY OF PERSONAL BRANDING

To know what qualities or characteristics your personal brand should reflect, you must consider the following. Think about a person you admire. What qualities of theirs make them admirable in your eyes? What qualities do you wish you possessed?

Then, know who you wish to impress. What is the end goal of this personal campaign? Is it a partner, school, or company? Again, find out what qualities make them desirable in your eyes. For example, if it is a company you wish to work for, what attracts you to it? Why do you want to apply? What values and visions of theirs do you find likable?

Next, think about any three qualities or traits you wish to be known for. What would you want the world to remember about you after you are gone? What impact do you wish to create? How would you like to be remembered?

Then, figure out how you want people to feel when they meet you. Should they feel warm or scared? Should they feel anxious or at ease? The qualities and values you treasure will have a certain impact on the ones around you. If you are too resilient in your own perspective, you might miss out on what others have to contribute. If your world revolves around only you, it might be a problem because others won't like it. Therefore, understand how you want others to feel around you. Ideally, they should feel welcomed, comfortable, and seen.

Next, focus on the story your clothes, appearance, and body language tells. If you were in a movie, what role would you be playing? How would you be dressed? How would you look appearance-wise? This is how you determine your heart's core wishes and possibly the things you wish to change about yourself.

Additionally, think about the values you have and be mindful of them when creating your personal brand portfolio. I wouldn't suggest anything that goes against your beliefs or practices. Ask trusted friends and family for feedback if required to get everything accurate and precise.

Interactive Element

Now that we know what personal branding is all about, let's put this knowledge to use. Let's create a personal brand portfolio style where you list your strengths and weaknesses and talk about the image you wish to present to the world, the kind of people you wish to attract, and what you are truly made of.

Exercise

Knowing Thyself

Answer the following questions about yourself to create
a strong personal brand:

Top three things I am good at.	1. 2. 3.
Top three things I wish I can improve.	1. 2. 3.
The most important thing in my life is ...	
The most important people in my life are...	
What success means to me.	
What's my superpower?	
What do I want others to see in me?	
Things I am afraid of.	
I am most stressed when...	
The achievement I am most proud of.	
The kind of impression I wish to leave.	
What do I want to be remembered for?	

Once you have a clearer picture of how you want to present yourself to the world, work on areas that need improvement. Suppose you listed poor communication skills as a weakness. Now is the time to work on that skill and turn it into a strength. Now, this might seem easier said than done, but identifying a problem is the first step to solving it. When it comes to creating a personal brand, if you know why people don't feel attracted to you or have positive things to say about you, this self-awareness exercise will remedy that. It will empower you to become the best version of yourself and make every interaction, new or old, more meaningful and engaging.

If you have made it this far, you are only going to love what's coming even more—the power of healthy, positive, and strong habits. Oh, I love talking about this and can't wait to share all that my brain has rounded up.

CHAPTER SUMMARY

2 Chapter Summary

Know what you, as a brand, have to offer. It is easy to be labeled as someone you are not. For others, you might be the life of the party, but in reality, you might be someone who hates all the **attention they get**.

KEY TAKEAWAYS

2 **Key Takeaways**

1. **Your values** should coincide with **your brand's personality.**
2. **To create lasting impressions,** you must have a strong personality, followed by an awareness of self as well as good traits and habits.
3. Put the **real "you"** out there to connect with people like yourself and share your life with them.

SUMMARY

Summary

We love to be the center of attention. We crave fame and reputation. But what we fail to realize is what we are putting out in the world. Oftentimes, our fame and value are only in our heads, while others aren't pleased with what we represent. In the second chapter, we looked at how perceptions originate about someone, the factors that go into creating a lasting first impression, and how we can develop a personal brand that is a representation of our values, good traits, and exceptional personality. Through various exercises, try to find the real **"YOU."** Additionally:

→ **Learn how you can create** an unforgettable first impression.Know what factors contribute to creating one. Can you maintain good eye contact? Do you dress well? Is your body language positive and welcoming? Are you smiling enough to attract like-minded people?

→ Furthermore, to create the persona of a **memorable "you,"** it is equally important that your values should align with your actions. Like any good brand, it should live up to the expectations it sets and deliver its promise.

LOOK AFTER YOUR MOST IMPORTANT ASSET – YOURSELF

 We first make our habits, and then our habits make us.

— JOHN DRYDEN

Ever wondered how precious your life is? As teenagers, we tend to be reckless, pumped up with adrenaline, with raging hormones telling us to be adventurous and just go out there. We seldom think about the value our life holds and how sacred the time we have is. We only have one chance to make it through before it all ends. So let me ask you this: Are you making the most of it?

Are you creating memories worth living? Are you leading a purposeful life? Are you at least trying to find out who you are (no pressure, though)? Or are you someone who is just letting one day go after the other, letting things happen to you? Are you someone who doesn't have any passions or goals to look forward to?

As important as knowing yourself and making a good impression on others is, you must also ensure that your life is well lived. Think about it, when was the last time you did something you were proud of? Like super proud of? When was the last time you felt alive and happy?

Shouldn't all your days be like that? Shouldn't they start on a high note and end on a high note too? Shouldn't every day be an amazing one?

Let's begin by ensuring that you take care of the most important asset: yourself. You are the reason for someone's smile. You are the reason for someone's support. You are the reason someone lives more happily and fully.

So are you taking care of yourself the way you should? Are you doing enough for your mind to function at its best, your body to perform at its peak, and your soul to feel enriched and wholesome? Are you putting in the hours to have a good night's sleep, eating nutrient-rich food, and drinking enough water?

These might seem like basic commandments everyone follows, but sometimes your efforts aren't enough.

Besides, who doesn't find going to a McDonald's or Starbucks easier than home cooking and juicing a glass of fresh oranges? There are days when we all feel like we don't have the strength to prepare home-cooked meals, but Taco Bell or Papa John's isn't always the answer to your hunger. I can go on and on about the harmful effects of fatty foods on your health but let me get straight to the point: You aren't doing yourself any favors by indulging in these. Preservatives and processed foods are the biggest culprits for increasing obesity percentages in the US and UK (Rauber et al., 2020). The pandemic did us no good, either. Although we did cut down on store-bought meals, it didn't stop our alcohol and cigarette consumption. The idle lifestyle, working from home, and poor sleeping schedules only made matters worse.

What you put in your body today will affect the amount of energy and bone density you have in your body ten or twenty years from now. If you don't exercise, your body will keep on losing its flexibility and form. It is not rocket science that gravity will do its work, and you will have a body that lacks any stability, form, or strength.

To emphasize the need for good eating habits and a healthy diet, did you know that more and more women today are having C-sections instead of natural deliveries? Ever wondered what the reason is? It's because many women's bodies lack the strength and flexibility women had a few decades ago. Women who are overweight (with a high body mass index ratio) are more likely to have a caesarian. This doesn't stop here. Children born via C-section are more likely to suffer an increased rate of diseases, such as type 1 diabetes, asthma, obesity, allergies, and reduced cognitive functioning.

This isn't to scare you but to give you a mental image of how some of us could end up bringing physically and cognitively weak babies into the world.

There is science about the dangers of poor eating habits, not just eating the wrong foods. The food you eat affects your sleep, mood, and stamina. It affects your focus and productivity. This is why you feel lethargic and sleepy after a heavy meal. It's your body shutting down and trying to cope with the additional pressure you have put on it. It has to break down the food, turn it into energy, and then metabolize it. Fatty foods, although delicious, contain fewer amounts of soluble fats. The energy levels are poor as well.

And this is just one aspect of taking care of your body. I haven't even gotten to the dangers of poor sleeping, lack of physical activity, and an unhealthy gut. Before we get to them and discuss more about the effects of a poor diet, let's understand how habits originate.

HOW HABITS ORIGINATE

In 2018's bestseller *Atomic Habits*, author James Clear writes that your life is a total of all your habits (Clear, 2018). The way you dress, the shape you are in, whether you are happy or unhappy, and so on, is a result of your habits. An action that you repeatedly do becomes a habit over time. It becomes a part of who you are. You don't have to think about it before doing it. It comes naturally, like brushing your teeth every morning. You just do it when you enter the bathroom first thing in the morning, even when you don't plan on eating anything anytime soon.

According to Clear, habits are formed on a four-step loop. Every habit, as simple as making noise while eating food or sitting at a designated table at school, has become a habit after it passes through the four steps.

First comes the cue. A cue is a trigger for the brain. It is what convinces it to initiate a behavior. It predicts the reward your brain finds tempting. Cues have long helped humankind to survive. Our ancestors could predict primary rewards like food, shelter, and water using these. For example, muddiness or wet soil indicated water nearby. Today, we use the same cues for secondary rewards like success and wealth. Our mind continuously analyzes our internal and external environment for cues that ultimately lead to rewards. A cue is the first indication or promise of a worthy reward.

The second step of the habit loop is cravings. Cravings can be defined as the motivation behind behaviors. Without motivation, we might not pay attention to the cues around us. For example, hunger is a cue. But if you don't act on it, you might never reach the second step where you start craving for certain food (reward) because of hunger. Without craving for change, we don't have any reason to act. Cravings aren't a habit but the change that they deliver. Brushing your teeth every morning isn't the craving but rather the feeling of a fresh and clean mouth. Similarly, you don't turn on the television just for fun; you do it because you want to be entertained. Every craving is tied to a desire to change the current state you are in.

What follows next is a response. The response is the actual action that takes place. It is the habit you perform. It is directly proportional to how motivated or unmotivated you are. But if the particular habit requires strenuous mental or physical effort, then you might be willing to expend it. In this case, you won't do it. The response also relies on how able you are. For example, if you have never thrown a ball in your life, wanting to play for the big leagues might sound like a passion, but it isn't possible without rigorous, continuous practice. Also, if you have a short height, dunking a basketball will be a challenge as you can't jump as high as someone with more height.

Response delivers the reward. After you are tempted by a cue/trigger and are motivated enough to actually respond to that cue or craving, the reward is the result. We chase rewards because they satisfy us. Rewards offer benefits that satisfy us. For example, hunger is fulfilled by food. A job means money, and money means you can get the things you desire.

Keep in mind that all four of these have to be a part of the habit loop. Without a cue, no behavior will initiate. Without a craving, you won't act. Without a response, there is no point in a craving. Eliminate the reward, and you will eliminate the response because you won't be motivated enough to act. Similarly, if the behavior is difficult to perform, your motivation will stumble. Eating healthy, for instance, might start off fine, especially when you have made it a New Year's resolution, but as you go on and find out how difficult it is to keep pace, you might lose the motivation. Furthermore, if healthy eating doesn't offer the quick fix you were after (the reward is unable to satisfy you), it will also not become a habit. Without all four, the behavior won't be repeated.

Every behavior is aimed at solving a problem. Most of the time, the problem is that you notice something desirable, and you want to have it. Take clothes on a mannequin in a shopping mall as an example. You want to wear it and look glam. That is a cue. You envision yourself wearing it and getting all the looks and praises for it. That's the reward. The cue registers motivation to either save or borrow money from your parents. Buying the dress becomes the response to that craving.

Other times, the problem is that you want to relieve feelings of pain. In this case, if you have recently suffered heartache, seeing other couples being all lovey-dovey might trigger the motivation to want the same or reduce the hurt it causes. Whatever action you take to feel better will be the response. Getting over the breakup will then become the reward.

Here's an idea: Think about a habit that you recently discovered about yourself. It could be listening to the radio when in the car, jumping steps on a staircase, or using your phone in bed. Can you recall how and when it all started? What behaviors led to it? Why were they repeated? Think about it and notice how easy it is to start a new habit without knowledge.

You may have missed out on the cues despite them being right in front of you, but your brain remembered. It remembered the pattern or order of things and turned it on automatically. Now, you repeat those behaviors unconsciously because they have become a part of who you are. Amazing, isn't it?

Now that we understand how habits form, let's quickly learn how we can start new ones and keep repeating the behaviors with the same motivation as Day 1 until they become a habit.

NEW HABITS . . . LOADING

Habits streamline and simplify lives. The right habits yield the results we want. When we repeat an action frequently, the brain requires little of the mental energy it required initially. But how can you create habits that stick? How can you avoid losing motivation? How do we make them an automatic part of our routines?

There are some practices to ensure that good habits stick. Always start small. You can't hike a mountain on your first try when you have never hiked before. Always aim to start small and consistently practice. For example, if the goal is to change your diet and eat healthily, don't expect to leave all junk food in a day. Start simple and small. Instead of munching on candies, go for almonds or peanuts instead. If the goal is to lose weight, start going to the gym. You don't need to do fifty push-ups on the first day. You can start with five and let your body adjust to the changes. If you start on a high or attempt to achieve everything in one week, you will likely fail, and it will destroy your morale too. Therefore, start small, stay consistent, and have patience.

Another fun way to stick to a new habit is to consistently perform the action for thirty days. Four to six weeks are enough to make a new habit automatic. Since the initial conditioning phase is the hardest, making it a 30-day challenge will keep you motivated and driven. It will also be easier to sustain momentum when you can track your progress.

Use the "but if I . . ." whenever you feel like you are losing morale. Using but at the end of every disheartening sentence is a great technique to overcome challenges and hurdles you think you can't overcome. It breeds motivation and willpower. Here are some examples of how it looks in practice.

- I will fail the exam this coming week because I haven't even started studying . . . but if I break down the coursework into smaller chunks, I can get most of it finished before the examination day.
- I don't know what to write in my college essay . . . but if I start noting down my strengths and weaknesses on paper, I can surely get a better idea of what I need to include and leave out.
- I can't balance work and life simultaneously . . . but if I learn how to prioritize better and manage time effectively, I know I will do better.

Notice how easily you can change a hopeless situation into a positive one?

Exercise

Can you come up with some situations you think are hopeless but aren't really? How about you use this technique and see what workable options you come up with?

	Problem	Solution
1		
2		
3		
4		
5		

Next, remove temptations from around you. If you want to eat healthily, you can't have junk food lying around the house. That's a temptation right there. Replace them with fruits or whole nuts so you can consume them when eating out of boredom. Similarly, if you are worried you are spending too much time on social media, how about going on a digital cleanse for a week?

Have someone on the journey with you. A buddy or partner will help you stay motivated and on track. If getting in shape is the goal, you can drag each other and hold each other accountable every day. Doing things together with a partner is also fun. You won't feel like quitting.

Also, if you continue to struggle with sticking to a new habit, find out what's stopping you. Could it be poor timing, lack of ability, or mental focus? Has the reward stopped being as tempting as before? Find out the reasons behind the excuses you make to yourself. A lot of times, just poor timing is the reason. You already have a lot going on in your life, and you stress yourself more by starting a new habit. Rethink and reassess. Address the issues and resolve them.

Set yourself up for success. Don't let excuses happen. For example, if you decide to go to the gym after school but forget to pick up your gym clothes, have your bag packed the night before and placed where you can't forget to pick it up. Similarly, if you are trying to adjust your sleep schedule, don't bring your phone to bed with you. You will only be tempted to use it.

Another important thing you must do is find something creative and engaging to do with the time you let go by idly. For example, if boredom makes you crave junk food, replace it with doing something creative and fun. This is especially helpful when you are trying to get rid of a bad habit like smoking. Don't let the triggers get to you. If you smoke during your free period, keep yourself busy during that time to not be reminded of needing to smoke.

Next, don't let a small failure get in the way of your goal. To say that you will stick with a new habit without any shortfalls is crazy. There will be days when you will feel like giving up and resorting to your old habits. Don't sweat it. The aim isn't to be perfect. It is to be consistent. Tell yourself that it is fine if you skip a workout, have a cheat day, or stay up late. Just be sure not to turn it into a ritual.

KEYSTONE HABITS TO START WITH

Sticking to good, healthy, and positive habits is the recipe to success in every walk of life. Whether it is a relationship, career, or personal goal, good habits are what make you achieve it. As teenagers, you might feel motivated to start a new habit. Although it is totally up to you to decide what habits you want to inculcate, some keystone habits serve as great starters.

Keystone habits are practices and routines that help us operate. They are the foundation for every habit we have taken after. Think of keystone habits as a default mode. These are what create a ripple effect. You start with a basic habit, and it goes on to serve as the basis for many others. One positive change has the potential to bring about other positive changes. Sleeping for an adequate seven to nine hours every night is a keystone habit. It leaves you feeling refreshed and recharged upon waking up. Feeling refreshed equates to better cognitive functioning, which translates to better ideas and creativity. See how one practice changes the way we do things?

Some keystone habits (like having family dinners every night) may not appear to have any significant change, but they do. When you gather around as a family at a dinner table, it has a big impact. Dinners allow healthy familial conversations to happen. Parents can know about their children's activities. Children can learn about how their parent's day went. Charles Duhigg (2012), a New York Times Bestseller and journalist, writes in his book, *The Power of Habit*, that families who eat together raise children with enhanced homework skills, higher grades, better emotional regulation, and confidence.

Similar to this keystone habit is making your bed early. There is a great short video of Admiral William H. McRaven (Texas Exes, 2014), where he speaks to the graduates of the University of Texas. He talks about his basic SEAL training, where his instructors would show up in the barracks room to inspect the beds. The young men in training were expected to make their bed every morning. They had to ensure all corners were square, the covers were pulled tight, and the pillows centered.

It seemed like a simple and mundane task to him, but years later, he realized how wise the practice was. You see, if the men made their beds perfectly first thing in the morning, they had already accomplished the first task of the day to perfection. It gave them a sense of pride and motivation to move on to the next task with more confidence. By the end of the day, one task turned into several accomplished tasks. Making the bed reinforced the idea that simple things in life matter. If you can't do them right, you won't be able to do the big things right.

Furthermore, if you had a miserable day, you still come back to a well-made bed, which refuels your lost motivation and gives you encouragement for a better tomorrow.

Remarkable, right?

Today, making your bed is linked with increased productivity, better budget skills, and a sense of well-being (Duhigg, 2012). Bedmakers are more likely to find jobs that suit them, own a house, feel well-rested, and exercise (Dutton, 2012).

Another keystone habit to include in your life is physical activity. You don't need to build muscle in a gym or run on a treadmill to lose excess fat; going on a jog, walking your dog, or doing some basic push-ups or planks also counts as a workout. Exercise makes people aware of what they put in their bodies. Suddenly they want to switch to easily digestible fats and low-calorie foods. People who exercise regularly also report reduced stress, more happiness, increased patience, and better productivity. Exercise also improves mood, sleep, and confidence (Harvard Health Publishing, 2019).

Speaking of eating, another thing you must build a habit of is tracking what you eat and drink. According to one study, participants who journalized their food journey lost twice as much weight as those who didn't (Hollis et al., 2008). This brings us to the importance of keeping track of how many calories you intake daily.

Meditation and mindfulness also come recommended as keystone habits. A short but composed meditation session allows the brain to be at peace and work through different thoughts one at a time. Meditation also leads to a strong immune system, increased memory and awareness, reduced blood pressure and anxiety, and so on. A clear mind translates to a productive, focused, and creative mind.

Finally, build the habit of planning your day and prioritizing the most important tasks. Start your day by sitting down for a few minutes to mentally visualize all the things you plan on doing. Prioritize them based on their importance. Leave out some gaps for breaks to relax the mind and to enjoy.

WHAT NEEDS TAKING CARE?

Apart from these keystone habits, there are several things you need to take care of. Remember how we talked about you being the most important asset? Now let's break that thought down and see what we can do to make the most of our abilities and skills. After all, we owe this to ourselves. Our mind, body, and soul do so much for us every day. A simple act such as walking won't be possible if our bones aren't capable of it. We can't feel at ease if our gut/digestion isn't satisfactory. Similarly, we can't feel happy if our heart is broken and hurt.

Like many others, taking care of your overall health is a vital life skill. Now that you are seeking that independence and trying to make it on your own, ensuring that you take care of your diet, hydration, physique, brain, and so on is crucial. You need to take responsibility for how you wish to proceed with self-care.

You can either be someone that takes everything for granted or use your abilities to become the best version of yourself.

Besides, it isn't as hard as everyone makes it out to be. Your independence relies on how well you can look after yourself without adult intervention. So let's take matters into our hands and see how we can do our best and be our best.

Your Diet

Let's start with your diet. Eating a balanced and healthy diet is one of the most important aspects of overall well-being. Eighty percent of premature cardiovascular diseases, such as a stroke can be prevented if your eating habits are healthy. A healthy diet prevents the accumulation of cholesterol in the body, which is the leading cause of heart attacks and obesity.

But what does a healthy diet mean? What should it include? Should you become a vegan?

A healthy diet is a diet that contains all the nutrients essential for healthy physical growth. These include proteins, carbohydrates, minerals, and vitamins. If you are looking for a short blueprint for a healthy diet and what it must include, take a look below.

Vegetables and Fruits

You already know this, but vegetables and fruits come packed with nutrients and vitamins no other foods can substitute for. They are rich in fiber, minerals, and antioxidants that help you maintain a healthy weight and satisfy your hunger. They are low in calories, leaving you feeling energetic and refreshed for a long while.

Some of the most important fruits and vegetables that come recommended by dieticians and nutritionists include:

- Blueberries.
- Citrus fruits like lemons, grapefruit, and oranges.
- Bananas.
- Avocados.

- Ginger.
- Garlic.
- Bell peppers.
- Tomatoes.
- Olives.
- Kale.
- Spinach.
- Cauliflower.
- Broccoli.
- Sweet potatoes.
- Carrots.

As a general rule of thumb, fill half of your plate with leafy greens and juicy fruits at every meal. Best if you consume them before your meal.

Whole Grains

Whole-grain foods are prepared using the entire grain, meaning its three parts are intact (bran, germ, and endosperm). They are high in fiber, iron, magnesium, manganese, vitamin B, and phosphorus. Whole grains include:

- Whole oats.
- Brown rice.
- Whole-grain rye.
- Whole wheat.
- Whole barley.
- Buckwheat.
- Millet.
- Quinoa.

It is best to opt for whole-grain pasta and bread over refined white bread. A quarter of your plate should be filled with these.

Protein

Protein is present in the bone, muscles, skin, hair, and tissue. Proteins make up the enzymes that drive many chemical reactions. It is made from 20+ amino acids (basic building blocks) that the body can't produce itself. Therefore, it has to rely on food from the outside to ensure the uninterrupted functioning of the body.

Protein helps repair body cells, regulate digestive processes, and is essential for healthy and balanced growth in children and teens. They maintain bone density, muscle strength, and prevent skin aging. A quarter of your plate should contain protein.

Healthy proteins include:

- Legumes, lentils, and beans like kidneys, chickpeas, lima, mung, and pinto.
- Seeds and nuts, including almonds, pistachios, walnuts, cashews, hazelnuts, chia seeds, and pecans.
- Whole eggs.
- Seafood like fish, mollusks, and crustaceans.
- Lean cuts of meats like unprocessed beef, lamb, veal, pork, and mutton.
- Poultry, including chicken, turkey, and duck.
- Dairy products, including soy beverages, low-fat milk, cottage cheese, fat-free yogurts, and low-fat cheeses.

So, this is what your plate should look like:

Your Hydration

Water makes up a significant proportion of our bodies. Despite being present in a large amount, water is lost in sweat and urine throughout the day. Some of it even leaks through our skin in the form of evaporation. There are differences of opinion when it comes to the amount of water one must intake. An adult should have at least six to eight glasses of water per day. However, if someone is engaged in some heavy physical activity and sweat gets lost from the body, they should drink more. Hot and cold weather also affects the amount. During winters, the body doesn't sweat as much as it does during hotter months. Therefore, the body retains more water. Athletes and gym enthusiasts must also drink more than most, as they lose more fluid during high-intensity workouts.

A well-hydrated individual can concentrate better, prevent their mouth from becoming dry, feel less fatigued, be more active, and have glowing and healthy skin. Dehydration can leave one feeling dizzy and light-headed. Water prevents health conditions like constipation and kidney infections. The more water you drink, the more flexible you will feel, as water acts as a lubricant and shock absorber between the joints.

Water should be consumed the way it is—no need to add any artificial flavors to it. Many people assume that fruit juices offer a substitute for water, but it isn't true. Although fruit juices do contain some essential minerals and vitamins, they aren't a substitute for water or fruits.

Also, carbonated drinks, as stated before, are a big no-no. I know it is hard to stay away from them when marketers and manufacturers want you to consume them as a substitute for water, but keep in mind that carbonated drinks have been linked to obesity, type 2 diabetes, and tooth decay. Every time you have a sugary carbonated drink, your stomach belches. This could easily lead to heartburn and a foul taste in your mouth. Drinks like Coca-Cola and Pepsi also weaken bone strength and density. The harmful effects don't end here. Research also links soft drinks to an increased risk of gout (Choi & Curhan, 2008), cancer, and cardiovascular diseases (Dagfinn, 2012).

So don't be fooled by the advertising for energy drinks, showing people your age having the time of their lives by surviving on them.

Your Exercise

According to CDC guidelines (U.S. Department of Health and Human Services, 2018), teenagers should engage in 60 minutes of moderate to vigorous aerobic exercise daily. Basically, aerobic exercise is any exercise that gets your heart pumping. Exercises like brisk walking, dancing, cycling, running, swimming, or roller skating are all forms of exercise that will keep you in shape and increase body flexibility and stamina. If you are a gym enthusiast, squats, strength training, push-ups, and planks are effective ways to stay fit and healthy.

You can also take part in your school's basketball or football team and remain in shape. The nature of these games requires that you adopt an active lifestyle, as it all comes down to how good you are on your feet.

If all this sounds like too much work, follow the shorter workout routines of your favorite athletes, and get going. There are tons of trainers on YouTube and Instagram who offer short workout routines on their channels and profiles. Just follow their lead and begin. Or you can create a customized home workout routine for yourself. Here are some basic exercise ideas for a 10-minute workout session:

- Start with some good warmup exercises. A good 2- to 3-minute stretch will warm up your body and muscles, preparing them for the upcoming round of exercises.
- Start with a set of squats (10 reps).
- Take a 10-second break.
- Then follow up with 10 push-ups.
- Again, rest for 10 seconds.
- Do some forward/backward lunges (10 reps for each leg).
- Allow yourself 20 seconds of resting time.
- Plank for 15 to 20 seconds (aim for more as you continue throughout the week).
- Rest for 10 seconds.
- Then end with jumping jacks (10 reps).

If this still doesn't get you enthusiastic, how about dancing to your favorite tunes freestyle or joining a 5K marathon? I am positive there is always something happening in the city you live in. Find them and get on board with them. Invite your friends to take part so that it becomes a fun activity.

Still struggling to adopt a healthy, physically active lifestyle? You can't say no to these ideas!

→ Walk to school every day instead of taking the bus.
→ Volunteer at your community center (for example, running errands).
→ Take a walk to your nearest park every weekend.
→ Do yard work for your neighbors, like cleaning their driveway, raking dead leaves, and pulling out weeds.
→ Help mom and dad with household chores like cleaning and organizing.
→ Take up a DIY project like assembling IKEA furniture or painting a wall.
→ When revising something, walk around the room.
→ Take your dog out for a walk.

Notice how these are simple yet effective ways to stay physically active? These require minimum effort on your part and still yield healthy results. Keep in mind that now is the time to build bone density, make your muscles flexible, and gain healthy stamina. If you continue with a healthy and active lifestyle, you will prevent becoming prey to a sedentary lifestyle later in life. When you become conscious about what it takes to burn only a few calories, you will also be watchful of what you eat and drink.

Your Sleep

Your sleep regulates every other function of your body. It sets the mood for the next day. It gives your brain some time to relax and recharge. It promises clarity of thought, high energy levels, and a well-rested body. However, this is only guaranteed when you sleep for at least five to seven hours every night on a schedule. But let's not forget that you guys are teenagers, and your phones are your best friends. Let's not forget that you would rather scroll through Instagram, send snaps, and make Tik Tok videos all night than sleep. Why waste time sleeping, right?

Wrong.

Catching up on what the world is doing shouldn't be second nature. Teen sleep deprivation is becoming a new pandemic no one was prepared for. It is an urgent health risk as more and more teenagers aren't getting enough sleep all night. According to Ellen Selkie, an M.D. and adolescent medicine physician, young children's bodies are still developing and growing (Mostafavi, 2018). Teenagers go through many hormonal and chemical changes in their bodies as they hit their teens, making sleep all the more important for their overall health and hormonal balance. Poor quality of sleep, or the lack of it, per se, affects teenagers' ability to function optimally and perform well at school. It eats off their concentration and focus and leaves them with problems like poor attention spans, lack of focus, anxiety, and even weight-related issues. Lack of sleep impacts their mood as well, which affects their relationships too.

Lack of sleep increases your chances of getting sick, which translates to more school days lost. It can also meddle with your driving skills, making you drowsy or fatigued. If you don't get quality sleep every night, you can expect to drift off mentally during the day, require short naps, make poor decisions, feel aggressive and moody, and have slow physical reflexes.

So how can you create good sleep habits? How can you manage both its quality and quantity? Let's learn together.

For starters, you need to be consistent with when you sleep every night. This means no breaks or laziness on weekends either. I know it seems a bit bland and boring to sleep at ten on the weekends when you should be partying with your friends or having sleepovers. But consistency is the key. That's how you can build a healthy habit of quality sleeping time. If you can't go to bed at ten on a Saturday because it feels unfair, try to sleep an hour later, max. This also goes for when you wake up. If you wake up at seven for school, follow the same routine for the weekends. Go on a hike, shop at a nearby store, or take up a DIY project to work on.

Second, don't take your phone to bed with you. Make sure your devices are turned off or on silent and placed away from your bed. You may have picked up the habit of listening to some music to sleep, but don't rely on the electronics to do that for you. Sleep is a natural body requirement unless you have a medical condition that affects it.

Take a hot bath before getting into bed. Hot showers help calm the body and muscles. The more relaxed you are, the better you will sleep.

Keep your room's temperature cool, preferably around 68°F. According to one study, sleep comes faster when the body feels a little chilly (Pacheco, 2023). It's harder to fall asleep when the temperature is hot.

Speaking of temperature, make sure that you black out the windows at night. Light and noise from the outside can ruin the quality of your sleep. You can keep a lamp on if you can't sleep without some light in the room but try to black out most of the light to trick your mind into thinking it is time to sleep.

Some eating habits affect how you sleep. For example, caffeine isn't a great idea a couple of hours before bedtime as it recharges you with a burst of energy. That doesn't just go for sipping on coffee; it also applies to sodas and snacks that come packed with it. Make it a habit to monitor your caffeine intake throughout the day and try to stick with having all of it before evening. If you crave something hot before bedtime, warm up some milk or herbal tea that promotes good sleep.

Additionally, don't make a habit of going to bed hungry or completely stuffed. Your stomach will remain upset or grumble. Heavy meals right before bed take longer to digest. This means your body is at work even three to four hours after the meal's consumption. In the end, your body doesn't get enough time to rest before you are up again and eating something new. On the contrary, when you go to bed hungry, starvation will keep you up or restless because the body lacks the fuel it needs to function optimally.

Another great tip is to not schedule appointments or classes right after waking up. If you have a class or training session to attend, schedule it a couple of hours after you wake up. Early morning appointments mean you will have to compromise your sleep if you don't sleep on time the night before. You will also have poor focus and attention.

I often tell my children to use their beds only for sleeping. Have a separate workstation or area for study and homework. Use your bed solely for sleeping so that when you are on it, the brain automatically associates it with sleeping time. I have also made it a rule to charge all electronics away from the bed. Yes, the socket right next to your bedside is tempting and easier to use. But if you use that to charge your phone, you will be tempted to use your phone more and more.

Avoid taking afternoon naps in the daytime. Small naps of 15 to 20 minutes are okay as long as they are before evening. Napping for too long or too close to your bedtime will make it difficult to fall asleep at bedtime because the body already feels relaxed after a nap.

During the daytime, try to get as much sunlight as possible, especially during the early morning hours. That is when the sun has sufficient vitamin D for you to absorb. Healthy exposure to sunlight or bright lights during the day keeps your body's internal clock on track. So spend some time outside during the day.

Lastly, manage your worries. One of the biggest reasons teenagers are sleep-deprived today is that they have too much going on in their lives, which results in anxiety and stress. Too much stress can disrupt your sleep quality and quantity. Use stress management techniques (discussed in the next chapter) to keep a hold of your concerns and have a peaceful sleep. If something continues to bother you, write it down on a piece of paper to have it out of your system. You can also meditate or consider deep breathing exercises to manage stress.

Your Gut

The microbiome is the foundation of your health. It refers to a group of up to 1,000 bacterial species that live in your small intestine. It is both good and bad bacteria. Good bacteria help destroy harmful bacteria, regulate digestion, and control your immune system. When we consume food, only a portion of it gets absorbed by our stomach's walls. The majority of the absorption happens in the small intestine. The gut bacteria break down nutrients essential for your body. It produces enzymes that promote the breakdown of indigestible carbo-hydrates.

For a healthy gut, you must have a balance between the good and bad bacteria in your digestive system. If your gut isn't healthy, your immunity decreases, hormones stop functioning, and you get sick often. Therefore, you must give your body a chance to feel healthy and function at its best by ensuring good gut health. Given the recent pandemic horror, the importance of healthy immune systems can't be stressed enough. Teenagers are a vulnerable group with poor eating and sleeping habits, and it becomes even more crucial to have strong immunity. So how can you promote a healthy gut, you ask? Take a look!

Stop relying on antibiotics for every small inconvenience. Got some allergies? Try herbal teas and aromatherapy. Got some nasal conges-tion? How about taking some steam and turning on a humidifier to purify the air in your room instead of some over-the-counter drugs? Although antibiotics save lives, they also impact your microbiome. They can take away your body's natural inclination to fight off bacteria and infections.

Lower your stress levels. Any form of distress or trauma, whether they are psychological, environmental, or physical, can disrupt the function and structure of your gut microbiome. Therefore, learn to manage your worries.

Quit smoking if you do. Smoking increases your chances of contracting chronic intestinal disorders and cancers.

Sleep six to eight hours every night. Good quality sleep can improve cognition, mood, and gut health. During one study on animals, irregular sleeping habits resulted in a decrease in the gut flora and increased the risk of inflammatory conditions (Voigt et al., 2014).

Check for food intolerances, if any. Some people aren't good at digesting certain foods. You may experience bloating, uneasiness, gas, or abdominal pain after eating a certain food (for example, milk). This is a sign that you have intolerance toward it and should consume less of it or have it in a state where its quantity is balanced by other foods. For example, you can consume it in a milkshake with fruits to tone down its effects. It's best to eliminate foods that are sure to cause you uneasiness as they are harmful to your gut.

To increase the number of good gut bacteria, try foods rich in probiotics. Kefir, yogurt, and fresh sauerkraut are examples of such foods. Add them to your diet and try to have at least one cup of yogurt (any kind) during the day.

Finally, make sure that you chew your food thoroughly and slowly. The more soluble your food is, the easier it will go down and be digested. Your body will require less time to break it down. Eating meals slowly and thoroughly also improves metabolism. When you eat slowly, your body will get tired of chewing and will signal the brain to stop. This means you will consume less of what you do now and prevent overeating or binge eating.

Your Heart

Taking care of your heart isn't just about eating healthy or getting enough exercise. Taking care of your heart also includes emotional care, preventing heartbreak, and being mentally and emotionally happy. Your heart is a cherished organ. It doesn't just pump blood all day. It communicates some important signals to the brain. For example, when you feel hurt, it signals to your brain to watch something cheery and light-hearted to stop feeling bad. When it is pumped up after a rigorous exercise session, it evokes feelings of happiness, improving your mood and boosting self-confidence. When it falls for someone, it makes you do crazy things—things you wouldn't do otherwise.

But that's how it is. Taking care of it surely should be at the top of your priorities. You must ensure it is happy and full of love and kindness. You must ensure it provokes positive thoughts and kindles positivity from the outside.

A happy heart is at peace with the universe. A person with a happy heart is content with what they have and experiences pure bliss. They know how to live a fulfilling life. They are gracious, compassionate, and empathetic. More happiness equates to less stress in life. Less stress means no anxiety or depression. Fewer worries mean more things to be grateful and appreciative of. Think of it as a chain of events only happening because you have positivity in your mind.

So how do you ensure it stays the way it is? How does it remain in its best shape and form? How does it perform optimally?

Be gracious. Be kind and compassionate. Find the best in things. Not all experiences will be good but view them as lessons to learn from. Be thankful for the little things in life, like good friends, caring parents, devoted teachers, and a loving community. Be thankful for the healthy food, a warm bed, and a secure place to call home. We often take these things for granted, never going about their importance in life. I know this because I move a lot due to work. I can tell you, in all honesty, that there is no place like home. You may vacation in the best of hotels, but the peaceful sleep you get in your own bed is the best of all.

Stay connected. Have a strong support system you can lean on. Strong friendships offer the emotional support you need to get through numerous teenage challenges. Be it a breakup, poor grades, or lack of social skills, your friends, parents, and educators can help you ace these challenges with their guidance, support, and presence. When you feel down, these supportive relationships will help your heart feel better and cared for.

Don't settle for something you don't deserve. Always seek the best because you deserve it. If you are in a relationship with someone who doesn't appreciate or value what you bring to the table, remove yourself from it. You are too young to be making important life decisions right now. You may think you have the best of the best, but don't let abuse be masked as possessiveness or care. Do not give yourself to someone who doesn't know how to value it. One way to protect your heart from getting hurt is by choosing the kind of relationships you want to be in and distancing yourself from the ones you don't want to be in. Some kids remain in toxic relationships because they are repeatedly told that they will be left alone and discarded if their partner leaves. Remove this thought from your head. An ideal partner shouldn't feel like a burden. They should be a companion, a lover, and a caretaker. You should feel more comfortable around them than stressed and afraid.

Besides, finding a partner to date shouldn't be on the agenda right now. What you should focus on are your values, goals, and morals. You should focus on securing a good future for yourself and gathering the right skills and tools for it. Eliminate people from your life who waste your time. Eliminate activities that add nothing to your skill set. Prioritize yourself and your dreams above all. Go after that scholarship that you wanted with full dedication. Work on your technique if you want to become a professional sportsman in college. Learn a new skill to boost your confidence and have a better chance at getting into your preferred colleges. Let your heart fulfill its desires to see you achieve your dreams. Nothing will make it happier.

Speaking of having clear goals, one of the best ways to do so is by practicing mindfulness. Mindfulness brings clarity. It is an act of being in the present, removing all unnecessary thoughts from your mind. It is about being in a state of peace with yourself without judgment. You sit with yourself, simply breathing. Whatever thoughts enter or leave the mind, you let them pass through you without labeling them as good or bad. They are, after all, just a part of you. That's what you tell yourself. They have no power unless you give it to them. Mindfulness calms your soul and your body.

While you eliminate toxic people and activities from your life, be sure to choose who you respond to and how. There will always be situations that will get the best of you, happen when you least expect them, and leave you blindsided. How you perceive them, learn from them, and move on is on you. It could be a pandemic, an illness, or failure—you have the power to decide how you move past these challenging times and what becomes of you. You can either react and lose all control or respond and act wisely. You can either be harsh or brutal with yourself and self-blame or be resilient and kind to yourself. The latter promises hope and peace for the heart.

To ensure your heart's sound health, find some time to do the things you love. Pick up a hobby you enjoyed not many years ago. Or, find a new interest altogether, like photography or landscaping. Find some time to unwind and focus on something relaxing and stress-relieving. Your mind and heart will thank you for it!

Don't forget to laugh, either. Today, you don't have to go to a standup show to enjoy some good humor. It's available just a click away. Tons and tons of content get uploaded every second from every part of the world. Is it a cat trying to have a leap of faith and jump? Or is it a dog wearing a suit of armor? Is it a man running into a pole or a teenager falling over a trash can? There is so much to remain entertained for hours and hours. Just make sure you find something that makes your heart smile too.

Your Mind

Caring for your body and heart is a lot easier than caring for your mind. It isn't something that one thinks of right off the bat, but your mind requires as much care as your heart and other organs. It is, after all, the powerhouse that looks after everything else. It is what makes a thought originate, then associates certain emotions with it, and triggers action. It regulates behavior and mood, ensuring that we feel a certain way in different situations. Imagine if it didn't have that insight. Imagine feeling sad on your happiest day or happiest on your saddest day. It even sounds stupid when you think about it. It registers pain and happiness and rushes to our aid when we need it. Try putting your hand on a burning candle. It's your brain's immediate response that prevents a burn, and you pull your hand back.

But we care the least about it. Why? It's because of the fears, thoughts, and uncomfortable emotions it houses.

We choose to avoid feeling pain or facing negative emotions. We are best at suppressing them, which is why taking care of our brains is the last thing we think about. But we need to learn to deal with them, push them away, and let them go. We need to learn to make peace with our thoughts and fears, acknowledge their existence, and then label them to better understand our reactions. It won't always be the most comfortable thing you do, but you must. You mustn't let distractions and noise prevent you from facing your fears and failures.

It may be the place where the darkest and twisted secrets reside, but it is also where we find our most beautiful memories. The time when your grandmother gifted you a quilted blanket you don't go to bed without, the time when you first built a treehouse, the time when you came in first in a race . . . there is so much to cherish and hold on to.

But if you neglect taking care of your mind, chances are you will forget them. Research tells us that to keep your brain performing at its best, it requires exercise and training (Ding et al., 2006). Think of it as a muscle. To keep it in shape and retain its flexibility, you must exercise it regularly. Here's how you can take care of your mind, face your fears, and deal with difficult emotions to ensure good health.

Start by carving some time out for your brain. Sit with your thoughts and analyze what's going on in your life. What thoughts crowd your mind? What worries bother you? What dreams do you have?

Meditation and yoga are great ways to declutter your mind. There is so much that doesn't need to be there. Through meditation and yoga, you can choose to focus on what's important, map out a plan to deal with it, and move on to the next thought or problem. Meditation is a structured way to reduce anxiety, stress, and depression while promoting relaxation. Luckily, you no longer need to take a yoga class to get started. There are tons and tons of online lessons, guided meditation tapes, and audiobooks that you can use to get started. You can even download apps and have a meditator guide you regarding the poses and techniques. Start with five minutes a day and see how amazing and relaxed you feel.

Next, go for a mental cleanse. Like a digital detox, a mental cleanse works the same way. You distance yourself from the very thing that harms you or is considered bad. Here, things like limiting beliefs, negative feelings, and bad habits are the ones you need to eliminate from your mind. But you have to do the work. Like any diet, it is on you to feed yourself good foods and limit the consumption of bad ones.

In a mental cleanse, you must feed your mind with positive ideas, thoughts, and feelings. You need to engage in habits that promote overall well-being, like getting a good night's sleep, staying hydrated, and prioritizing things. A mental cleanse also includes shifting your focus from the things out of your control to the ones in your control. This means you can only prepare yourself for an interview. You can't determine the outcome. Whether you land the job or not is purely out of your control. Therefore, there's no point in stressing over things you have no control over. You must also establish healthy boundaries so that toxic people and habits don't consume your brain. Your time and energy are limited. You must learn to invest it in people and habits worth the time.

Keep in mind that a mental cleanse isn't just about embracing all that's good. You eliminate the bad but also acknowledge its presence and impact. Why do you feel scared? What emotions does it evoke? How can you channel your emotions and behaviors better? A mental cleanse should help you focus on that, too.

Challenge your brain to keep it alert and active. Engage in new activities frequently. Don't let your brain go dull. Keep it challenged by learning new skills. Learning something new or doing something creative requires imagination and problem-solving skills. Take doing a puzzle, for example. There are so many pieces, and each piece can only go in one spot. For the picture to come alive, you must find that place and put it there. It is your brain's job to find the right place and join all the pieces together. Similarly, you can keep your brain sharp by revisiting an old skill, like playing an instrument you used to play when you were younger. You can also learn a new word every day or try learning a new sport or language. There are countless challenges if you decide to go that route. Doing this will also make you fearless, as everything will seem possible.

As for those pent-up feelings and emotions that you don't want to sit with, find creative outlets to express them and get them out of your system and mind. Things like journaling, drawing, or painting are excellent examples of expressing your feelings comfortably. You can also try writing poetry or song lyrics to talk about how you feel. The idea is to channel your emotional state through mediums of art. You don't need to be an artist or perfectionist to do that. Just start!

As important as it is for your heart to be surrounded by dear ones, so it is for your brain. Research tells us that meeting with friends, discussing daily life, and sharing details about past events that you are still trying to process prevents burnout (Krasner et al., 2009). Supportive friends are, therefore, valuable for your mind too. You can talk things through and have worries leave your mind for good.

Journaling and brain dumping is another great way to keep your mind cleansed. Remember how we talked about eliminating mental clutter? This is another prime example of it. Brain dumping is a self-care practice for the mind. You start by putting your thoughts, fears, and worries to paper and then identifying the emotions they trigger. For example, if you are worried about a test result, it might evoke fear of failure, a decline in your self-confidence, and anxiety about the future. Now that you know and come to terms with these emotions, you can gain better clarity on how you wish to cope with them.

In Chapter 4, I shall discuss how to get started with a brain-dumping exercise/journaling to help organize your thoughts, label your feelings, and strategize on how you wish to cope with them. For now, let's learn how we can take care of our soul, the part that makes us who we are.

Your Soul

Your soul is the very essence of who you are. It is your deepest sense of self, an immaterial part of you. Your spirit, as you commonly hear, isn't just related to a certain belief or religion. It isn't just about attending religious sermons or studying texts and scriptures. It isn't all just linked to a Divine being. A spiritual connection is a connection with yourself. It involves becoming aware of who you are physically and then connecting that with your immaterial and immortal being. The connection, however, should be sincere and holy. It can't be of deceit and dishonesty. Your soul is connected to you the same way food is to your health. You can't live without it. Every food you eat or abstain from has an effect on you. The right foods give you strength, energy, and nutrients. The bad foods replenish it all and make you lazy, fatigued, and idle. The same is the case with your soul. What you feed it is what it will thrive on. Good habits, thoughts, and feelings promote happiness, while bad habits and emotions ignite negativity.

How spiritually connected you are with yourself determines your mood, gives you a purpose to look forward to, adds meaning to your life, connects you with yourself and others, and reminds you of all the good there is in the world.

While researching for this soul-enriching experience, I stumbled upon some simple ways to feel spiritually enlightened and connected with yourself, and I can't wait to share them with you. After reading these, I started following many of them, and trust me when I tell you this: I haven't felt more connected with the world, people, and God Himself than I do today. I am positive you will feel the same way as you incorporate these simple yet meaningful habits into your life to have a happy soul.

Talk to yourself as you would talk to a friend. Let's face it; we are our worst enemies. We are the first to put ourselves down when something goes wrong, drowning in self-pity and guilt. If only we aren't this dumb, we tell ourselves. But jeez, let's stop right there and think for a second. If a friend had committed the same blunder, would we be this harsh and critical of them? Would we have pointed out their stupidity or consoled them? Then, why don't we treat ourselves the same? Why aren't we kind to ourselves? Surely, we can do better and remind ourselves that we tried our best, no? The next time you are about to beat yourself up over something, I want you to stand in front of a mirror and say what you would say to a friend. Be compassionate and empathetic.

To find something to feel happy about every time you go out, make it a quest to spot at least five beautiful things around you. It could be a smiling baby, a man walking his dog, or a butterfly showing off its beautiful colors in a park. It could be the stunning sunset, a uniquely painted car, or a wall mural you can't take your eyes off. It could be someone dressed in a Joker costume or someone playing an instrument to earn a few coins. Let's call it a beauty scavenger hunt. When you go home, recall those things, and feel joyous about how beautiful the world around you is.

Another way to feel more connected with yourself and the people around you is to let chivalry win. Act like a gentleman/woman and help a stranger. See an old woman carrying multiple bags? Volunteer to help her and place them in her car. If you think your neighbor could use some help with the weed pulling, lend a hand. Open a door for a teacher, sit with a lonely kid at lunch, and become friends with them. There is so much you can do to brighten up someone's day. Always remember: A good deed never goes unnoticed. It always comes back. Besides, the joy of helping others is an unmatched emotion. You can't trade it for anything.

Check in with yourself daily. What is going on? How are you feeling? Sit quietly with your emotions and feelings without judgment. You don't need to feel overwhelmed. You simply must acknowledge their presence. Sitting with your feelings will make things a bit more realistic and clearer for you. You will feel much lighter and at ease once you acknowledge your emotions, feelings, and fears.

Pick who you want to spend your time with wisely. Choose who you wish to follow and unfollow, who inspires you, and who doesn't, whose company makes you feel wholesome, and whose doesn't. Some people are radiators, while others are drainers. Radiators emit hope, enthusiasm, and positivity. They are all about seeing the glass half full. There is never a dull moment with such people. They bring with them a ray of sunshine and beauty. Drainers, on the other hand, will put you down, remind you of your failures, and rob your energy. They are pessimists who look down upon everyone, including themselves.

If you really want to make your heart, mind, and soul happy, splurge a little. Buy something for yourself. Indulge in a self-care practice like enjoying a massage at a luxurious spa, watching your favorite team play, going to a concert, or buying a dress for yourself. Save up and take yourself on a date. Enjoy a delicious meal in your own company and see how amazing it feels to pamper yourself like this. Whenever I feel the need to do something for myself, I go to my favorite ice cream shop, all alone, and get their biggest Sundae to splurge on. Nothing tops that!

Repeat truth-filled affirmations to yourself daily. Consciously emit positivity and hope. The universe will respond with the same. Positive affirmations allow us to stay calm and hope for the best. We anticipate, in all truthfulness, that we deserve the best. Then, we leave that thought out there in the universe and hope that similar thoughts join and come back to us in the form of opportunities and ideas. These opportunities and ideas are what make our dreams come true.

Interactive Element

Now that you understand the importance of taking care of your body, health, mind, and soul, here's a fun activity I want you to take part in.

Let's say you are about fourteen or sixteen currently. Visualize yourself being ten years older. Now imagine that person looking at you. Do you think that person will be proud of you for who you are now? Do you think they will wish you had been more dedicated to your mental and physical well-being? Do you think that person will be happy about the decisions you make right now? What will they think of you carelessly wasting your time over celebrities who don't even know you? What will they think if you want to be like Samantha from class, the most popular girl in high school, or Nathan, a soccer star? Do you think that person would wish you were just you?

Let this ten-year-older you hold you accountable for your actions and casualness. Let this person be your guide and mentor. Surely, you want to be successful, right? Surely, you want everyone to see you as a wise human being. Surely, you want more freedom and control of your life. But are you putting in the work that's required to gain that freedom? Are you being responsible and accountable for your actions and activities? Are you spending your time wisely? Are you picking up the skills that will help you achieve your dream goal in life?

If not, it's something you must think about because ten years from now, you won't have the same passion, time, and energy to start something new. I know people say that you are a forever learner but let me tell you this: When you grow older and are supposed to have your life figured out, there is little room for error. You get fewer shots to make blunders because expectations grow higher. You are supposed to act like an adult the moment you move out and start on your own. There is no pressure, per se, but society won't let you off the hook so easily. Right now, you can make mistakes and learn from them because you still have a home to come back to and parents who can provide for you. But when you are on your own, you have to think about these additional expenses too.

So let's simplify this problem by creating a list of habits and behaviors you wish to address in your current life. Set a timeline, say six months or a year, to change habits that do you no good and behaviors that get you in trouble.

A year is an ideal time to change and reset a bad habit. It is also an ideal time to adopt a new behavior. For example, sleeping in late is a bad habit that affects all areas of your life, from your grades to your mood. Try changing that. Similarly, anger can be a behavior on your list that you wish to get rid of. I want you to list strategies or ideas that you will use to change those habits and behaviors. Let me demonstrate it with a few examples, and then you can pick it up from there.

Exercise

Habits / Behaviors	Strategies/Coping Mechanism
Junk food addiction	→ Account for calories in everything. → Munch on almonds, peanuts, and walnuts instead. → Differentiate between boredom and hunger. → Be mindful while eating. → Take smaller bites and chew more.
Wasting money on unnecessary things	→ Make a monthly/weekly budget to prioritize important/unimportant expenses. → Put excess money in a savings account. → Look up investment options. → Save for college expenses.
Guilt-tripping / being too harsh on yourself	→ Set clear expectations for yourself. → Have clearly defined goals and action plans. → Take responsibility for emotions and feelings. → Practice gratitude and empathy.
Tantrums / meltdowns	→ Know your triggers. → Engage in deep breathing exercises/ relaxation techniques. → Redirect and distract yourself. → Release anger by removing yourself from the situation.
	→
	→

Now, you go ahead and make a list of your own and see what habits and behaviors you come up with. Also, try to start with one habit or behavior at a time when trying to change or reset it. You can't take on more than what you can handle. Let one habit reset, and then move on to the next. Remember, slow and steady wins the race.

Exercise

Habit/Behavior Transformation: 30-Day Challenge

Start a **30-day challenge** to change that habit and see how you fare. Cross off each day that you succeed in staying true to the new habit or behavior and let it become your new norm. Here's a template to get you started.

MON	TUE	WED	THU	FRI	SAT	SUN
1	2	3	4	5	6	7
8	9	10	11	12	13	14
15	16	17	18	19	20	21
22	23	24	25	26	27	28
29	30					

Optional: You can add notes and appreciation remarks if you like.

This is how you start self-care management. You put in the effort and harvest the results you want. Only when you can take care of your physical self can you take the responsibility of moving out and living on your own. Remember, these are the very basic life skills that you must learn to get by easily. But this isn't all.

There is something far more important or at least equally important than taking care of your physical well-being. Emotional and mental well-being—they call it. Sadly, this isn't something they taught at school when we were young. Today, school administrations are more involved in ensuring the mental well-being of their students and go the extra mile by hiring counselors and therapists to help students who need it. Timely recognition is the first step. The sooner a mental health issue is diagnosed, the better.

Therefore, let's learn how you can improve your mental well-being and feel emotionally content. Let's learn and discuss coping strategies to help you get out of any challenging situation stress-free and with self-confidence.

CHAPTER SUMMARY

 3 Chapter Summary

The importance of building strong habits, eliminating bad ones, and self-care practices to ensure you put your best self out there. An emphasis on good dietary and hydration habits as well as proper sleep and mental well-being have also remained an integral theme of this chapter.

KEY TAKEAWAYS

Key Takeaways

1. How habits originate, and what **roles our values** and beliefs play in building them.

2. How to **form new and better habits** to ensure good health, improved hygiene, and excellent productivity.

3. **Healthy exercises for your body, mind,** and **soul** to achieve the desired focus, along with a 30-day challenge to eliminate a bad habit and instill a good one.

SUMMARY

 # Summary

Healthy habits are the keystone for success in life. When it comes to preparing a teenager for adulthood, it is these habits that determine how successful or unsuccessful they will be. This chapter explores their origin as well as how to instill good habits. It also discovers the many aspects that teenagers must take control of in their lives, such as:

→ **Consuming a healthy and balanced diet**, as well as the importance of staying hydrated.

→ **Making physical activity** a part of your daily routines to ensure strong bones and flexible stature.

→ **Having a good sleep routine** and how to improve the quality of your sleep.

→ **Taking care of your gut** by staying away from alcohol and smoking.

→ **Caring for your heart** by staying connected, eliminating toxic people, and being grateful and positive about your future.

→ **Learning how to reframe negative thoughts** and stay resilient in the face of adversity.

→ **Enriching the soul** with new experiences to become more aware of your passions and purpose in life.

No One Is Alone

"Do what you can, with what you have, where you are."

— *THEODORE ROOSEVELT*

For some reason, even though every teenager out there thinks about impending adulthood with as much fear as they do excitement for the freedom it brings, it isn't something anyone talks about. It was the same when I was a teenager too – and the reason back then was the same as it is now.

People rarely feel comfortable talking about what scares them. We don't want to feel weak, and we worry that, somehow, everyone else already has it all figured out. Plus, since they don't teach us about survival in the adult world at school, it isn't a part of everyday conversation.

It should be – and I think if it was, we'd all feel far less scared of it, and we wouldn't feel ashamed of the worries we have. You might not think any of your friends are worrying about this stuff, but trust me: They are.

I wrote this book to try to help as many people like you as I can. This is a stage we all have to go through, and I want you to be able to walk confidently into adulthood, ready to enjoy all of its blessings without having to worry about how to handle the hard parts. And now that you're on this journey with me, I'd like to ask for your help in reaching more of the young people who might be reluctant to admit that they're scared too.

By leaving a review of this book on Amazon, you'll show other teenagers that they're not alone in their fears – and that there's a way for them to skill up and become a true titan as they transition into adulthood.

Your review will show new readers exactly where they can find all the guidance they hardly dare admit they're looking for... Just like you have.

Thank you so much for your support. Much as they may try to hide it, this is something every teenager worries about, and it warms my heart that you're willing to help them.

Scan the QR code to leave your review on Amazon.

(If you're feeling creative, snap a photo of your favorite chapter or a cozy reading nook and share it with your review).

4

MANAGING YOURSELF

> *Every human has four endowments—self-awareness, conscience, independent will, and creative imagination. These give us the ultimate human freedom . . . The power to choose, to respond, to change.*

— STEPHEN COVEY

S elf-awareness, as Covey believes, gives us the power to be who we are, practice what we want, and change what we dislike about ourselves. It may sound simple, but it is one of the most difficult kinds of life skills. Not everyone can see themselves in a negative light. It takes courage to do that.

Why?

It's because you might come across things and habits that aren't positive or suitable. You may come across habits and thoughts that have been negatively affecting you. Take procrastination, for example. If you have the habit of delaying things until the last minute, you know what it costs you. Working on a project the night before the submission date doesn't always go as planned. Something might come up, disrupting your plans to submit your project on time, and then getting your marks deducted.

This is acceptable once or twice, but if you have built a habit of deliberately putting things off, it is something that must be addressed. Only when you are aware that this is a problem can you address it. This awareness is what looking deep within yourself offers.

It takes strength to sit with your thoughts, declutter, and organize them. You need to be humble and kind to yourself too. Doing so will allow you to be with yourself without any judgment or discomfort. Through self-awareness, you can regulate your internal condition and cause a ripple effect. If we continue with the procrastination example, acknowledging that it is there will trigger a ripple effect where you seek to amend to overcome it. Once you overcome it, you will start to notice the positive impacts it has. You will feel relaxed when you have things in order. There will be no panic or anxiety regarding the project. You will have time to revise and improve it however you like, something which isn't possible when you attempt things last minute.

Self-awareness can challenge your thoughts, sense of self, and behavior. It can introduce you to attributes that aren't pleasant but present within you. For example, you may find lying an easy way to get out of troublesome situations. But if you know that's a habit you need to discourage, you will feel challenged to change it.

Self-awareness also empowers you to manage your emotions and feelings well. Right now, this seems like the most important thing to do, given the many hormonal changes you are going through. Puberty is hard for everyone. You don't know what's going on with your body, mood, or feelings. Some days you feel like crying all day, cuddled up in your bed, while on others, you want to be out and about. It is no secret that your thoughts and feelings regulate your actions and behaviors. The right thoughts will fuel the right motivation, whereas wrong thoughts will yield wrong actions. Therefore, recognizing how you feel inside and what thoughts trigger certain behaviors and actions is crucial.

According to a study on self-awareness by the Eurich group, researchers concluded that when individuals look inward, they can better clarify their values, feelings, thoughts, strengths, weaknesses, and behaviors (Fletcher & Bailey, 2003). They can also recognize the impact they have on others based on how well or poorly they know themselves. Most self-aware people have happier and more fulfilling relationships. They experience a sense of social and personal control in their lives (Ridley et al., 1992). They also seem more satisfied with their careers as they know what they are doing and why.

Another study suggests that people who can see themselves clearly are more creative and confident (Silvia & O'Brien, 2004). Self-aware people are also good at making important decisions and can communicate and advocate for themselves more effectively (Sutton et al., 2015). They know what they want and how to get it. When they can see inside themselves, they understand what their core values are. They ensure they don't have to compromise on them and, therefore, are outspoken, confident, and courageous. The same people can easily put themselves in others' shoes because they know how others perceive them or what they expect from them.

Yet, so many of us remain unaware and thoughtless about the impact our thoughts have on us. Within each of us is a tremendous opportunity to create change. But how can we when we fear knowing ourselves?

Self-awareness and introspection empower us to know what we want out of this limited time we have on earth and to make the most of it. Imagine living a life without purpose or awareness. Imagine yourself sitting behind a desk, working for a cause you don't care about. Isn't that wasting your time and energy? Isn't the thought depressing? What if I tell you that you might end up the same if you don't know what your true cause in life is?

The benefits of self-awareness are vast. Your personal growth is tied to you. How much or little control you have over your life and decisions about you depends on it. You can improve your mental health by knowing what thoughts trouble you and finding ways to ditch them. You can develop stronger relationships when you know what you seek in a partner and what values you want your relationships to be based on.

The biggest advantage, however, remains your ability to manage your thoughts and emotions, aka yourself. You are a sum of all the thoughts you have that trigger an action or habit. If you have that control, imagine the things you can do or change. If any negative feeling arises, you can recognize it instantly and take the necessary steps to improve your mental state. But if you don't know what's bothering you, you will keep guessing and wasting time without actually doing anything about it.

OBSERVE AND FEEL – YOUR NEW MANTRA

Your sight and ability to feel things either spiritually, emotionally, or physically are remarkable blessings. Through your eyes, you can view, interpret, and take in new information. Through your ability to feel, you can make sense of that newfound information and use it as you like. These senses, combined, dictate actions and behaviors.

Thoughts, like breathing, are automatic. But we can make them deliberate by focusing on something particular. Think of it like molding a sculpture into the desired shape. It starts with wet clay, and then through precision, dedication, and commitment, it becomes a distinguishable shape, has an identity, and makes you feel things. Similarly, if we take a thought and combine it with similar thoughts, we can trigger an action or build a desired habit. Isn't it a gift to be cherished?

But let's not forget that the hands that shape the sculpture do it with motivation. Your thoughts need guidance too. The mind needs precision, focus, and dedication. You can't reap the fruits without getting your hands dirty. This stands as the only challenge between you and your goal to manage your actions and reactions.

But what about the thoughts that enter the mind without permission? What about the ones that randomly step into our mind's realm without notice or intention? Those are the ones that we need to disregard. Those are the ones that we need to eliminate so that we can focus on the ones we want to focus on.

We think all the time. Even when we tell ourselves to stop, we can't. Moreover, it is hard to let go of thought once it has entered the mind. Even when you tell your mind to stop thinking about it, it can't. Don't believe me? Let's do an experiment. Think about your favorite food joint. What is that one thing that you always get from their menu? Visualize the taste, aroma, and feel of it in your hands.

Now stop thinking about it immediately.

Think about literally anything else but that item.

Quit it.

Did you succeed? Probably not. You are still thinking about it as you read this, despite me repeatedly telling you not to.

So how do you deal with your emotions and reactions to those thoughts or feelings when you can't even control them? Surely, they are going to overrule every other positive thought you have or want to have.

Processing and interpretation are the key. You must process them, interpret their real goal, and then work out strategies to either keep focusing on them or let go. Interesting, but how? Let's learn.

PROCESSING AND INTERPRETATION

Emotions and feelings are a part of our lives. They set up the mood, make us enjoy a moment to the fullest, and grieve when going through a difficult time. Smiles, laughter, crying, or anger are all emotions that we experience routinely. Sometimes, they come coupled with feelings like jealousy, envy, pride, or anxiety. To some extent, it is our emotions that control our actions. But only when we allow them to!

For most people, especially as young as yourself, emotions can be a mystery. They can sometimes be confusing to interpret or name, let alone express. But the goal should be to express them as constructively as possible, even when they are the toughest to deal with. Constructive expression prevents conflicts, heartbreaks, and arguments, ensuring relationships don't lose their sanctity.

Negative emotions like sadness, fear, or anger are what most teenagers struggle with. With uncertain times ahead and unclear future plans, fear, worry, and even frustration can linger. It seems tempting to act upon them when they arise. You may want to cry, scream, or have the urge to break things because you struggle to deal with them healthily. But let's not forget that it doesn't resolve the pending issue. Or does it? What good has ever come from acting on your emotions other than feeling a little lighter? Anger doesn't fix anything. Fixing only begins when you get past that anger and think things through. Sometimes, the way we act leads to more trouble in the future. Some common ways teenagers are known to deal with their negative emotions include:

Denial: Refusing to accept the outcome of something solely because it doesn't align with the one you had in mind. Refusal to accept reality is a common theme these days. It is, after all, the hardest emotion. Denial keeps things at peace. It doesn't distort the fictional story you have been telling yourself. But denying your problematic feelings or bottling them up only ends with a full-blown meltdown or explosion. Some teenagers have a hard time coping with a breakup, but they pretend to be fine. Unresolved hurt then makes them do stupid things like hooking up with the wrong people, trying to make their ex jealous, or engaging in self-harm.

Withdrawal: Disengaging yourself from the situation or person you don't want to be around. This isn't as simple as wanting to spend some time alone but rather purposely avoiding something or someone. Withdrawal can be a sign of early depression too. When you decide you don't want to be around people or deal with your problems, it is because you lack the energy it requires, or you don't want to waste it on them. Your situation makes you overwhelmed. Sometimes, you withdraw when you feel that others take you for granted. Sometimes, it is because of a certain behavior of yours that you feel ashamed of and thus decide to isolate. Unfortunately, withdrawal brings along other problems like miscommunication, misunderstandings, distorted thinking, anger, and so on.

Self-harm: Self-harm is an alarming side effect when one feels reluctant to deal with negative feelings and emotions. It can take several forms, from cutting yourself, starvation, binging, and others. It can even include taking part in dangerous activities in the disguise of adventure. When you try to self-harm, you deliberately try to inflict pain on yourself for something you feel guilty over. Some feel self-harm gives them more control over their lives and how they choose to live them. But this form of temporary relief doesn't resolve the mental issue you face. In fact, it only makes you more addicted to them. There comes a point when the same problems you were trying to forget become the reason to provide momentary relief.

Substance abuse: Another common way teenagers like to forget about their negative emotions is through drugs and alcohol. Drugs have the tendency to numb the pain, at least for some time. In the long run, however, both alcohol and substance usage has been linked to brain damage. And let's not forget drunk driving and its drawbacks. Driving when you are not in your senses doesn't only risk your life; it risks the lives of everyone who's trying to get by in their lives. Nobody deserves to lose their life to a drunk driver who couldn't think of a better way to deal with their problems.

What to Do Instead?

The good news, however, is that you don't have to rely on any of these to get your emotions and feelings processed and interpreted. There are several other methods to process every positive or negative thought in a way that doesn't stop you in your tracks. This means they shouldn't trigger an unplanned and unwise reaction that will make matters worse. Emotional management is a life skill that will help you prosper in all walks of life. Be it your career, relationships, or new independence, how well you control your emotions from getting the best of you is how your success will be determined.

Think about it: Suppose you have an anger management issue. Picture yourself as a management head supervising a team of employees. Some days, some employees will mess up, test your patience, or leave you shocked. How will you cope with them and manage them if you can't control your anger outbursts? If you keep losing your cool over every small thing, how can the company expect you to manage your team and targets?

Similarly, if you suffer from anxiety, every small upset will lead to a panic attack, leaving you with sweaty palms, an unclear mind, and chaos. On the same note, if you can't manage your emotions appropriately, any relationship you enter will bring about challenges that you will find difficult to deal with.

Therefore, it is crucial that you learn to regulate your emotions in healthy and constructive ways.

All it takes is how you view and acknowledge them. Here are some exercises to better deal with any uneasy emotion or feeling that has you overwhelmed at the moment:

Exercise

Take your emotional temperature. Ask yourself the following questions to understand what the thought is about and what it is trying to evoke.

→ What feelings do I feel that I am aware of?
→ Which is the strongest among them?
(It could be fear, anger, or irritation).
→ How did I become aware of this feeling? (Did you react in a certain way to know it exists? If it was fear, did you start to sweat, feel panicked, or anxious?)

Answer these three questions in a calm state. Write down your answers for better clarity and expression.
Describe each feeling thoroughly, its impact, and its reason.
Let these answers guide you in better deciphering how you feel and why.

Next, identify the triggers/stressors. **What caused it in the first place?** Inquire the following:

→ Was there a situation or person that triggered it?
→ Is it happening because of a daily occurrence or nonoccurrence? (**Presence or absence of something.**)

Here, you might not have any concrete answers, so don't panic. Let the thought pass through you without judgment. Don't assume the worst. Wait for an outcome or response. You don't have to respond to all the thoughts you have. You don't need to pay attention to them if they confuse you. If you can, identify them. If you can't, don't waste your time on them.

Staying confused and unsure may make things harder, but that is where you can count on your supportive friends, colleagues, or partner. When we share our fears or anxieties with a loved one, they diminish in size. Suddenly, they seem reachable. The more we stifle a thought, the bigger it gets. Don't let that pressure cook, hit the timer, and become a bigger noise in your head than it should. Release the pressure gently and often with the closest of your kin. It's like a muscle spasm. The more you neglect your pain, the more persistent it becomes.

Exercise

Or, if you want a quicker and more practical version of the same approach, try walking the **PATH**.

1. **P**ause
2. **A**cknowledge
3. **T**hink
4. **H**elp

Pause: Pause is the **first step** before acting on any feeling or emotion. **Stop and think about your plan of action.** Take a minute to really allow the feeling or emotion to sink in before reacting to it. Perhaps, try counting to 10?

Acknowledge: In this step, you come to terms with what you are feeling. Are you mad at someone? **Do you feel sad or depressed about something?** Acknowledge that feeling and tell yourself that it's okay to feel that way.

Think: Now that you have allowed yourself to cool down and assess, **think about ways you can make yourself feel better.** For example, if you are mad at someone, perhaps leaving the room might help calm things.

Help: This is the part where you actually. Put into motion the practice you thought about in the third step. **Here are some ways you can help yourself feel better**, no matter what you are feeling.

→ Watch a funny YouTube video
→ Listen to some music
→ Play with a pet
→ Reorganize your room
→ Create a bucket list of places you wish to travel to
→ Eat a snack
→ Take a hot shower
→ Meditate
→ Take a nap
→ Rip a piece of paper into small pieces
→ Make a gratitude list
→ Cry or scream

STAYING CALM AMIDST THE CHAOS

While you try to manage yourself and your emotions, there will be times when you will feel like your patience and calm are slipping away. Anxiety will get the best of you, leaving you with uncomfortable feelings. This kind of stress puts the body into fight-or-flight mode, a tactic that releases chemicals designed to get you in a position to either fight or run away. This was more understandable when cavemen used the tactic to either run and hide from a wild animal or fight it. Today, the fear before getting on a stage to perform might not pose the same danger as a wild animal, but the stress is still the same. If you constantly find yourself worried about everything, it means that your fight-or-flight mode is easily triggered.

Even adults can't escape worries and anxieties. But unlike you, they have experience in handling stress and coping with anxiety. Many have mastered keeping their feelings and emotions from taking charge and can manage their emotions well. So how do you keep your cool and not lose your mind over every little thing? Asking that to a teenager whose body is basically ruled by their hormones might not be the best thing.

Let's look for some practical advice from experts who have studied, researched, and experimented with relaxation techniques to overcome a state of panic.

Inhale-Exhale

Researching the benefits and impacts of deep and slow breathing, Andrea Zaccaro, along with her colleagues, believes that slow and deep breathing triggers the body's natural response to release stress hormones and bring the body into a state of calm (Zaccaro et al., 2018). Focusing on your breathing also distracts the mind, promising some relaxation. Deep breathing is similar to beginner meditation.

1. You begin by slowly taking a deep breath through your nose, allowing it to go all the way to your belly.
2. Then, you hold on for a moment and then slowly exhale the air through your mouth.
3. You repeat the same process, increasing the time between each breath and fully immersing in it.

A simple one to three minutes of this practice can miraculously calm you down, normalize blood pressure, and relax your muscles.

Focus on the Positives

There are several cognitive distortions where our mind quickly jumps to the worst-case scenario in everything. We catastrophize simple problems, magnify them, and cause ourselves unsolicited panic and anxiety. It might not seem as simple as it sounds but hear me out: focus on the positive. Did you fail an exam? Focus on the fact that while preparing for it, you learned so many new things. Lose a game? Focus on the amount of fun and thrill you had playing it. Got cheated on? Focus on how you are better off without a disloyal partner. Believe it or not, there is always some silver lining. There is always some good that comes out of a bad situation. Every failure in life comes with a reward—called a lesson. You learn about the mistakes you made, improve, and restrategize, ensuring your success the next time.

Focusing on the positive will keep your mind in relaxed mode.

Challenge Negative Thoughts

Irrational thoughts are the reason you feel so anxious or angry most of the time. They don't always make sense, but they do amplify anxiety. One thought leads to another, and together, they can cause havoc. For example, one painful experience in the present day might mix with all your previous painful experiences and make you feel overwhelmed. You might end up saying things like, "I am cursed or something," "Luck is never on my side," or "I always screw up!"

Exercise

Challenge these thoughts. Don't give in to them and go back to thinking the worst. Break the cycle by logically assessing your situation. **How do you do that?**

Ask yourself the following questions:

→ Is it in my head or likely to happen?
→ Am I overthinking and generalizing things?
→ Does it happen to me often?
→ What is the worst that can happen, and how will I handle it?

Having a plan of action combined with a fighting spirit will make any irrational thoughts go away and relieve anxiety. Once you are past the stage of answering these questions, reframe your thinking. For example, if you are worried that a new partner will break your heart like your ex, try telling yourself that you are smart enough to see the red flags before getting too serious and are willing to give this new love a chance.

Take a Stroll

When feeling anxious or overwhelmed, try going for a walk in the open air. Run if you can. Both these activities are known to release the good chemicals that uplift mood and reduce cortisol (the stress hormone) in the body. Be it anger or frustration, release it by punching a wall or screaming in a secure environment. Doing so will help you feel lighter and clearer in the head.

Visualize Being Calm

Visualization is a powerful tool. It involves picturing, like really picturing yourself doing the things you want to do and succeeding at them. For example, if it is a difficult emotion you are dealing with, try visualizing freeing yourself from it, and feel the calm that takes over. You can also take deep breaths while you do so to release anxiety and stress. By creating a mental picture of being calm and feeling how it feels, you can begin to anticipate it too.

Shift Your Focus

If your emotions are getting the best of you, try distancing yourself from the place, situation, or people. Request to seek some air or time to process things and not let your emotions overwhelm you. It is true that we never make sound choices or rational decisions when we are enslaved by our emotions. This works when your life is in danger, and you have to think quickly. However, in everyday situations, when the danger isn't as imminent, it is best to rationalize things by giving yourself some time to think things over.

Try finding a centering object or person you can lean on when feeling overwhelmed. It could be a stuffed animal, a friend, a parent, or a pet. It can also be a stress ball you keep in your pocket for times when you feel anxious. Every time something bad happens, tell yourself to get in touch with that person or thing to calm you.

Chew Gum

It's as simple as that. Chewing gum is a practice that requires focus and attention. It keeps you focused on the present rather than delving into irrational thoughts. Chewing gum boosts productivity and mood. It helps relieve anxiety.

Retrain Your Brain

Life can be tough at times. It can throw problems at you that you don't feel capable of handling. To cope with them and stay calm in pressuring-inducing situations, learn to deal with stress healthily. Start with a growth mindset. Every time you feel stressed or over-whelmed, remind yourself that you may not have the skills, wisdom, or experience to deal with it now, but you will have it soon. There is no end to how much you can learn and master. So put a halt to your worrying thoughts by enforcing the idea that you aren't bothered because you know you have the power to overcome everything.

If things still feel out of control, tell yourself that you tried your best and gave it your best shot. If not today, you will succeed tomorrow.

BABY, ARE YOU DOWN (5X)

When anxiety and emotional regulation becomes difficult, it can turn into depression. Teenage depression is a growing concern today. According to data from 2017 alone, around 3.2 million teenagers aged 12 to 17 have depressive episodes (National Institute of Mental Health, 2022). In 2021, Mental Health America (n.d.-b) reported that major depression among youth has risen from 9.2% to 9.7% in just a year. Rates of depression are highest among individuals aged 18 to 25, but if the condition exists and no therapy or treatment has been sought, it can turn into chronic depression. Depression is also the cause of about two-thirds of suicides reported each year in the US alone (Valentine, 1999).

Surprisingly, not many people know they are depressed because the symptoms can vary from one person to another. In some people, the signs are self-explanatory, like persistent sadness, hopelessness, and difficulty showing interest in activities they once enjoyed. But for some, the symptoms might show up as difficulty concentrating, having a hard time taking care of themselves, irritation, body aches, a change in sleeping patterns, appetite, and so on.

These symptoms are the ones hardest to decode as they can mean many things. Poor focus and attention don't always mean one is depressed. It can also mean poor interest and intention. Similarly, an increase or decrease in appetite can translate to an underlying medical condition like stress and worry about an exam, a partner, or the future in general.

As a teenager, when you already have so much on your plate, talking about this additional concern with someone can be challenging. But you know what I always say? Acknowledgment is the first step to changing it. When you talk to someone about how you feel mentally and emotionally, you have already surpassed the first and most difficult hurdle. What remains next is getting treated for it.

When you're already managing the challenging emotions associated with depression, acknowledging the condition, and opening up to someone can feel difficult. But overcoming this challenge is how you begin the treatment.

You can talk to a teacher, school counselor, parent, or doctor about it. They can then involve more people like your parents, a therapist, or a psychologist to delve deeper into the issue and recommend the best treatment early on.

Feeling depressed can make you helpless. You may lose the will to fight back and just accept your reality. A diagnosis doesn't mean the end of the world. It doesn't mean there isn't much to do other than take medications or go for therapy. You can turn things around if you want to.

Starting with a healthy diet, proper sleep, and exercise, you can, once again, experience happiness and joy. Just some basic changes to your routine and diet will drastically alter the way you feel. Remember how we talked about the importance of these in Chapter 3? Remember how they all can improve mood, promote happiness, and reduce stress?

Well, apart from that, there are some other things you can do to come out of your current mental state where everything is gloomy and dark. Let's look at some natural treatments to improve your energy levels and an interest in the things you do (Griffin, n.d.).

Craft a routine: Depressed individuals can do well when they have a planned and busy day scheduled. When there is so much to do, your mind doesn't have time to wander to senseless thoughts. Depression strips away the structure from your life. Your challenge is to keep going, one task after the other, one day after the other, and one month after the other. An intentional daily routine will motivate you every time you finish off tasks successfully.

Set goals: Goal setting is another way to beat depression. When you have clear goals and deadlines, you have something to look forward to and focus your mind on. You may feel you lack the motivation to accomplish anything but still try. Start with goal setting to get your mind prepared. The goals don't have to be difficult. A goal can be taking a walk outside for ten minutes every morning. You might say it is such a simple goal, but for someone battling depression, the idea of leaving the house is a task itself, let alone going for a walk and meeting people. Therefore, always start small and make progress.

Volunteer to take responsibility: If you are living with your parents, ask them to assign you duties that will keep your mind distracted and focused elsewhere. It is natural to want to pull back from life when you are depressed. Having a responsibility that others hold you accountable for makes you do it.

Challenge difficult thoughts: Fight them with all your might. Give your brain reasons to ditch the thought because you are certain about your ability to conquer it. When you are depressed, a lot of the fight you must do is mental. It is easier to assume the worst than do something to change the way you feel. The next time you feel terrible and overwhelmed with emotions, question the very thought that's causing the ruckus. If the thought says no one likes you, counter it with a statement like, how can I be sure? Beat negative thoughts before they take control.

Stop dwelling on problems: It is good that you want to share your problems with a friend or a teacher but don't make it the only topic to talk about. Depressed people can indulge in guilt, self-blame, and a victim mentality. They can exploit problems too much. When you indulge in your problems too much, you only focus on the negative side of things. You can't see the positive, let alone believe it. Therefore, the next time you are out with a friend or loved one and airing your thoughts, talk about the positives too. Ask them to identify the positives if you have a hard time identifying them.

NEEDS MANAGEMENT

An important aspect of emotional and self-management involves having a voice. Advocating your needs and seeking help when you think you need it shouldn't be as hard as people make it to be. Knowing and voicing your needs pack several benefits. According to an article published in Psychology Today, Seth J. Gillihan, author and researcher, explains that those who can identify their needs are more likely to have them met (Gillihan, 2015). They also have better relationships and a greater sense of self, purpose, and freedom in their actions. They are emotionally stable, don't have a fear of missing out (FOMO), and have stability in work and relationships because they aren't wasting time wondering if they need something else entirely.

Asking for help shouldn't be hard. It is a means to introduce yourself to the things you are unaware of, unskilled at, or unable to grasp on your own. The rebellious teenager in you might want to do everything on its own, but seeking help isn't an act of weakness. It is an acknowledgment where you let the other person know that they are more experienced to provide input. Besides, you needed help all your childhood—with walking, feeding, talking, and homework when you started school. So why stop now? Surely the ones who care about you and want to see you succeed won't think of you as weak. They will be happy to provide feedback.

Coming back to needs fulfillment, here are some perks to asking for your needs and why.

Things are changing and will keep changing. Take a look around you and see how things are rapidly changing by the minute. LED screens have made chunky old TV boxes obsolete. Schools have new and improved curricula and courses. Newer and more improved versions of your favorite apps keep popping up, making your life easier. Take the pandemic as an example. See how those two years of social isolation changed the way we work, meet, and keep friends, notice how it changed our lifestyles? Notice how nature became more beautiful because of fewer CO_2 emissions and footprints? All in a span of fewer than two years?

The world will continue to change, and we can't know for certain how that will make us feel or affect us. In the phase you are in right now, nothing is certain. Your partner may change, you may start a new job, get a place of your own, or leave town for better opportunities. You'll need all the mental and emotional help with that.

Second, not asking for help when we need it pulls us away from life and relationships. We worry that if we ask our partner for a little inconvenience, they will feel burdened. We worry they will reject us, hold a grudge against us, and not understand where we are coming from. This isn't the case. Be it a partner, parent, or friend, we all want to make things easier for our loved ones. If that means compromising a little, we will be happy to. But you have to ask first.

You may feel left behind or isolated if you don't ask for help to fulfill your needs. We all want to feel loved, emotionally connected, and appreciated. What's the shame in asking for it, then? If everyone craves that, surely others around you will mirror the same sentiment. Speak up and request. For needs you can't fulfill yourself, it is best to have someone involved. After all, our needs make us human.

Asking for your needs or wants is also the only way you will reach your full potential. No one succeeds alone. We all need companionship, wisdom, and the opinion of others different from us to know if we are on the right path or not. Take any big organization or company. It isn't just one man's brilliance or effort. A whole division is involved in the production, advertising, and distribution of a product.

But all of this is only possible when you know what you need. You may think you are too young to have your whole life figured out for you. True. But you must have a vision. You must have some goals you look forward to achieving. You must know your needs so that others don't ignore them.

Exercise

Clarifying your needs is a must. Let me help you get started. Answer the following questions to help with what you currently need. Remember, your goals, passions, and interests will keep changing. So this isn't a **"forever kind"** of needs clarification list. Reassess your goals and interests every few months to know if you still love the things you once loved before:

1. Am I okay with the way I take care of myself currently?

2. What activities/passions/interests make me feel fulfilled and happy?

3. Where do I feel starved or empty? (Areas where you can do with some additional guidance and help.) Where do I feel I should invest my time and energy?

4. Do I have any activities or passions that calm me down? (Name any three.)

5. How much time do I give those activities?

6. What are the three things that bring me joy? (Activities, people, or interests.)

7. What activities and behaviors am I saying yes to, even though I would like to let go of them?

8. What activities and behaviors am I saying no to, even though I would like to adopt them?

9. Am I setting the right boundaries for myself to protect my time and energy?

10. What more can I do?

11. What do I wish I had done more of at the end of the day?

Once you have your answers, I want you to take a 30-day challenge where you ask for help from others. Challenge yourself not to feel ashamed when asking for help for something you deserve or need. This shouldn't be hard. It could mean a ton of things like asking for directions, a quick chit-chat over the phone, some pictures, guidance about career choices, feedback, or a hug. Just do it for thirty days in a row so that you eliminate any shyness or anxiety you feel before reaching out to someone.

How to Do It?

The #1 reason we hesitate to ask for help from someone is that we are deeply ingrained to mistake help for a favor. Asking for help isn't a favor. Get rid of this mental pattern that reminds you that every time you ask someone for something, you are being selfish, weak, or manipulative. You have to let go of the fear of rejection that ties to it. Asking for help doesn't equate to asking for a favor.

So how can you do it in a way that is acceptable and practical? How can you ask for help with something you need without feeling ashamed, selfish, or vulnerable? Here are a few tips:

Articulate Your Needs

One of the hardest things when asking someone for something is how the request has been worded. Am I being too pushy and manipulative? Do I sound vulnerable and weak? What tone should I go with? What words should I choose? I hope I don't offend them . . .

These are some of the most common thoughts you might stumble upon. Sometimes, you don't even know what you are asking for. Is it their time, pity, or consideration? Here's how you can better articulate your thoughts and words:

Be curious: What is it you truly need? Ask yourself this as if you were asking a friend about their needs. Be considerate and empathetic. Dialogue with your inner self and identify what you seek.

Build an Emotional Vocabulary

The signs we receive, or the answers we get, aren't always crystal clear when we try to identify our needs. Sometimes, we mistake them for something else. For example, it is easy to mistake appreciation for validation. Appreciation is praise for something you did well, and validation is just approval and acceptance. There is a minor difference between the two, but you can easily mistake it for the other. Sadly, our culture doesn't have a wide range of words to describe our emotions and feelings either. We have to move past words like sad, depressed, or anxious. We have to introduce broader and more explorative terms like feeling unseen, unappreciated, lonely, and neglected. For example, you may think you are feeling anger when in reality, you are frustrated, feeling wronged, victimized, or disappointed. You may feel taken for granted, which evokes similar emotions and feelings as anger.

- **Learn the difference between a need and a want:** These two words are often used interchangeably, but they differ in meaning. A need comes before a want. When all your needs are met, then you can move toward a want. A need is a more urgent desire. A want is supplementary. For example, you may think you want money, but what you really need is financial stability. You may think you want fame, but what your heart really desires is to be recognized and appreciated. If you have a sibling whom you wish would help clean the room, what you really mean is for them to contribute more. When you can clearly express your needs, people will begin to take you more seriously because needs can't be ignored. They may be delayed but never neglected. Without your needs being fulfilled, you can't experience true happiness. Wants are often connected to sudden feelings and temptations, like wanting an ice cream, going to a party, or buying that pretty dress you saw online.

Needs linger for a while and build slowly, like hunger. Therefore, separate your needs from wants and articulate them wisely.

- **Phone a friend:** Sometimes, you won't be able to name a need right away. You will experience sadness but not know why. You will feel depressed but fail to interpret your emotions. This is where a friend, counselor, parent, or therapist comes in. Ask them to help you identify what you are feeling. Maybe tell them the symptoms, and they can better label it for you. A simple conversation starter such as "Hey, I don't know why I feel sad all of a sudden. Can you help me try to figure out what's bothering me?" will go a long way and get the job done.

Learn How to Deliver

Any communication, whether verbal or nonverbal, isn't complete without two people acknowledging its understanding. Sometimes, it is our delivery, the way we say things, and the pitch and tone that we use that change the context. We are either too dominating that the context changes to being manipulative or too lenient that others don't take it seriously. You have to find a balance between the two so that you don't come off as too pushy or too lazy.

Emotions need to be expressed, feelings felt, and words communicated. Any feeling or emotion that remains bottled up for too long starts to brew and overfill your emotional pot. If you experience intense bouts of emotions, say anger or sadness, learn to communicate it in a way that is pleasant and not nonchalant. Communicate those emotions and then ask for what will make you feel better. You don't have to do it right away. Your message gets lost if you are yelling at someone, sobbing, or making personal remarks.

Your timing matters: Pick a time comfortable for both of you. The other person should be in a stable mental state to receive your information. Are you talking about your needs to a parent who has just come home, frustrated about the traffic on the road? They won't be able to hear or understand what you are saying because their mind is saturated. Let them cool off a little or decide on a time (perhaps a weekend) when you can voice your concerns with them. Similarly, if your roommate has just pulled an all-nighter, asking them to share chores around the house isn't the right time to bring it up.

Always begin the conversation by appreciating the person you are speaking to for something they do. Starting from a place of appreciation makes the other person more alert and interested. Starting with a sentence that instantaneously puts them on a pedestal may anger or hurt them. Create a sense of invitation where the receiver doesn't feel judged.

Be specific about your needs: Vagueness won't get you what you need. Clarity in communication is important to understand and interpret. Be specific about your needs. For example, if you want your parents to start seeing you as a grown-up individual, instead of saying "Why do you always compare me with others," say, "I wish you could see how much I have grown and learned. I hope you can acknowledge that and treat me as an equal." Use the same tone and consideration toward yourself too. Instead of labeling yourself as a failure, remind yourself that you just need to work harder the next time and learn from your mistakes. That's how you bring change.

Don't attack the person: If you aren't satisfied in a relationship, think that your parents don't understand you well, or feel judged by a professor at school, try to address their behavior and not them. When trying to clear things up with them, communicate how their actions made you feel rather than blatantly attacking them. Again, the idea is to focus on the behavior that you don't appreciate rather than pointing fingers at someone. If you continue with the latter, your needs will go unheard and unattended.

Interactive Element

Knowing how you feel, sitting with that feeling, and acknowledging its existence is the first step to healthily recovering from it. How can you do that? In modern times, a mood tracker is a tool to keep a record of your feelings at regular intervals. The goal is to help identify patterns and triggers that change your mood in different situations and circumstances. This works exceptionally well for adults with mental health issues, unable to cope with them. It is also best for those who experience anxiety or panic but don't know what triggers it. With a mood tracker, not only can you track your mood, but you can also regulate it. For example, perhaps you experience anxiety most before a strict teacher's class. You can note that in the mood tracker tool and then work out ways to manage it.

You can track your mood in a journal, create a mood chart, or use an app to note down information about your mood throughout the day.

Mood trackers help you identify factors that make you moody, anxious, stressed, or sad. You can use it to target unwanted behaviors or actions that you feel compelled to resort to whenever you battle a certain emotion. For instance, you might want to stay grounded at home, in your room, whenever there is a big party among your friends because you are an introvert and don't want to be a part of all the gossiping and rumors that happen there. You may leave texts "on read" and not communicate how you feel and why. This isn't what you call coping with it.

With a mood tracking tool, you can also learn how your diet, lifestyle, sleep, and different activities affect your mood. On days when you haven't had the best rest, you are bound to feel on edge because your brain isn't fully recharged to take in any new information and store it.

A mood tracker will also work as a prediction tool to prepare you for certain situations that lead to negative emotions and to help you avoid/cope with them constructively. With a mood tracker tool, you will feel more attuned to the factors that benefit or worsen your mental health and seek therapy (if required) before your emotional and mental state worsens.

You can rely on several options like mood tracker charts, mood tracker journals, or, the most popular choice, mood tracking apps.

While mood tracking journals that you can record daily are a good option, it isn't a very modern method. Think about it: You are always on your phone; you might as well track your mood. If you have reminders for drinking water and tracking how many calories you burn by walking throughout the day, why not add one that tracks your mood too? The same is the case with mood charts. They are reliable but a bit old-fashioned. But the upside, however, is that they are easy to access and get your hands on. You can use a DIY one at home with a few emoticon printouts and create a customized chart. You can also download a print-ready version right off the internet and track your mood for a week or a month. But since you run short on time most days, mood tracker apps are a good choice to stay up to date and not worry about any previous records or data. Mood tracking apps allow you to create a profile and set notifications at different intervals of the day to track your mood. Most apps are user-friendly and basic to begin with.

Another advantage is that you can also track and make notes of when you are happy or at peace. For example, something exciting happens and takes you by surprise. You can record that information about your sudden mood change right then and there on your phone. You won't have to go home and add that to your mood chart or journalize it. This ease of access makes it a suitable choice for teenagers such as yourself. If you keep track of the things that bring you joy, you can rely on those activities whenever you are feeling down or upset. They will become your coping methods during troubled times.

Mood tracking apps make mood tracking fun and interesting. It isn't like a chart that you have to fill out at the end of the day. It would feel like another task, and you won't be your most honest when doing it.

Suppose you feel lethargic or irritated about something, you won't be able to jot down how you honestly felt throughout the day.

Exercise

Take a minute to download a basic but reliable mood tracking app like MoodFit, Daylio, MoodKit, and more. **Create a profile and start tracking your mood by putting in the first entry. Set reminders for when you want to track your mood next.** For example, you can make your first entry at breakfast before going to school, during break time, after school, and then around evening and before going to bed.

Once you are done taking care of yourself and your emotional health, let's move on to something more complex and important that you will have to deal with every day of your life. Let's learn how to problem-solve, prioritize problems, and make peace with what you have no control over. In the final chapter, we shall look at how it's okay to make mistakes and not let them define you. Instead, what matters is how to take accountability for them and learn from them.

CHAPTER SUMMARY

 ## Chapter Summary

Your emotional growth and care are as crucial as your physical and mental health. This chapter focuses on how you can garner a **positive mindset** by working on your thoughts and turning them from negative to positive. It gives readers insights into how they can process and interpret various emotions they feel and find healthy ways to cope with them.

KEY TAKEAWAYS

 ## Key Takeaways

1. **Your thoughts play a key role** in shaping your emotions. The way you perceive things sets the pace for action.
2. Taking your **emotional temperature** from time to time helps you stay in the right mindset. You can learn the difference between being rational and being overwhelmed.
3. **Putting yourself first** should be the motto if you want your needs managed and your body and mind in excellent condition.

SUMMARY

 # Summary

Teenagers are stampeded with all sorts of emotions. First, they are going through several hormonal changes that open up a can of emotional irregularities. They are irritated, want more freedom, and are fed up with how quickly everything is changing. In addition to that, there is the stress of a scary world out there and how competitive they have to be to fit in. This usually takes a toll on their mental health, where they feel incapable of expressing what they are going through. This chapter addresses the following with a special focus on emotional and needs management. To summarize, we have talked about:

→ The importance of **self-awareness** to understand your emotional needs.

→ **The power of observation**, interpretation, and processing of a diverse range of emotions.

→ **Challenging negative emotions** by reframing thoughts, having a positive outlook, and having a growth mindset.

→ **Battling depression and anxiety by setting goals**, finding the time to do things that matter, and focusing on solutions instead of problems.

→ **Managing your needs**, no matter the kind, by being expressive and articulate about them.

HOW TO NIP IT IN THE BUD

 Expect problems and eat them for breakfast.

— ALFRED A. MONTAPERT

Change is an inevitable reality. You can either choose to accept that or remain grounded in your old and outdated ideas. Consider yourself as an example. Did you always have the same taste in music you have today? Do you still have the same fashion sense you had three years ago? Are you still into wearing your jeans at your lowest or wearing crop tops to school? Look at how much you have grown in the past few years.

Today, the world is changing faster than ever. From new filters introduced every day to new ways of doing things, your generation doesn't let things retire the way they should. It's something today and the opposite the next day. You must have come across videos where people are shocked when they find out they have been using something the wrong way their entire life. There are new ways of contouring your face, collarbone, and even your abs to fake a six-pack.

The world keeps changing, but are you? How are you coping with these changes? Does it make you stressed, or do you enjoy trying new things? Most of us believe that we are fine with change but aren't really. I know this because not long ago when I used to go grocery shopping, I would have the entire cart filled up and still pay only a decent amount for it. Today, I get five things, and the total is higher.

It bothers me a little, but I have to make peace with the change because it is the same everywhere. But let's not talk about inflation. Let's talk about the fact that whether you like it or not, you have to keep moving and accepting change.

The good news: If you have great problem-solving skills, it won't be a problem for you.

You will make peace, you will progress, and you will transform. You will master any skill or excel at anything you put your mind to if you are open to trying new ways of doing things. This requires that you learn to step out of your comfort zone.

GETTING OKAY WITH A CHANGING WORLD

What is a comfort zone? A comfort zone is a limitation you set for yourself, something you are happy with. This is a line beyond which things get tougher, and let's be honest; you don't want to put in the extra work. A comfort zone is defined as a psychological state where you feel at ease because you aren't being tested. It's like going to a restaurant and ordering the same item from the menu over and over again. You are afraid that trying something new won't always be a win. You are afraid you will have to change your eating habits or challenge your taste buds. So you stick with what you know and leave out the rest. Why? Because a familiar taste makes you feel in control.

The same applies to a job or environment. Most of us don't want to step out of our comfort zones because we feel stressed and anxious. We fear the uncertainty a new challenge comes with. We fear the failure and humiliation that will follow if we fail. And let's not blame it on ourselves; we have been designed that way.

It is a premeditated model. Humans have been made to fear uncertainty. We have been designed to avoid unnecessary risks and stay within the lines. No wonder it has modeled our behaviors too. Our ancestors, the cavemen, weren't considered the smartest when they let their curiosity wander. It is what got most of them killed until they came up with more efficient means to hunt, heal, and find shelter.

So why should we try to step outside of our comfort zones?

To sum it up in plain words: for personal growth. You have to step out to grow and learn new things. You have to step out for better opportunities. You have to step out to know what you are made of and how far you can go. How else would you know? Think of your comfort zone as standing at the bottom of a hill. You don't want to hike even though the landscapes and views promised to you are panoramic and out of this world. How will you know if you don't take the first step and then the second? How else will you bask in the views if you don't give yourself a chance to witness it yourself?

Many of us have lived an unfulfilling and unsatisfied life only because we were too afraid to step out. We felt burned out, lacked focus, and detested what we did . . . yet we never had the guts to explore the many options there were.

Let's make a pact to venture out and see what else there is in the world for you to explore. Let's promise not to let an unfulfilling career or relationship take over our lives and waste it. Let's vow to keep taking calculated risks and take on new challenges to know of the greatness we are made of.

Why? Because the world is changing faster than you can imagine! You need to be flexible to adapt, or else you will be left behind. All you need is to take baby steps and see what feels comfortable. For instance, if you wish to venture into standup comedy, how about writing a few jokes and trying out a set at a local bar? You may or may not be booed. But what if you succeed? What if you make an excellent impression and garner attention? It only takes a day to get viral these days. What if you are the next big star? But let's not get ahead of ourselves here. Baby steps, remember? Take things one day at a time.

Exercise

Here's an actionable 7-day step-out-of-your-comfort-zone approach:

Day 1: Do one thing you have always wanted to do

Your to-do list might have many unchecked items. Try shortening it by actually checking some of them off. Start with one thing, particularly something you find challenging or dread doing. It can be something as simple as planting a seed or as complex as learning a new language.

Day 2: Try a new exercise regime

Every guy or gal your age should exercise. Any form of physical activity will keep you in high spirits and good health as exercising releases the feel-good hormones and alleviates stress. Maybe try a new workout routine or take a new route for a jog. You can even challenge yourself to run an extra mile to test your limit.

Day 3: Change your routine

Are you living a robotic life where you get up and head to school? Then you come home and spend the remaining hours before sleep glued to the screen? Try doing something different for a change. For example, if you study from home most days, how about trying a different location? Perhaps something a bit more crowded or noisy. You can test your level of focus, attentiveness, and productivity.

Day 4: Travel somewhere new

This doesn't imply that you leave town for a day but rather change your usual views.

Aren't you tired of being stuck at the same traffic signal every day or passing by the same Wendy's? How about traveling for fun? You can go to a park, prepare a picnic basket, and eat in the open while watching the sun go down. The idea is to break away from your cemented travel route and give your eyes something new to look at.

Day 5: Choose a fear and face it
Everything we have been taught about being brave has been wrong. Being brave doesn't mean overcoming your fears or eliminating them. It is about moving forward despite them. Surely, the reason you are in a state of comfort is that you are holding yourself back. Start small. Face one fear. Challenge it and see what happens.

Day 6: Expand your skill set
As learned before, comfort zones prevent personal and professional growth. Are you getting too comfortable doing something you are overqualified for? Aim to gain a competitive edge over others and learn something new. Build your skill set using the resources you have. Doing so will make you a more competent contender in your industry.

Day 7: Celebrate
This day will be all about celebration. You might have failed to deliver in a couple of days or think you could have done better, but let's forget about it. Reframe your negative thoughts with positivity. Acknowledge the progress you made, regardless of how small it is. Treat yourself to a sweet delicacy of your liking or buy yourself a cute outfit. This will motivate you to continue making progress and stepping out of your comfort zone.

The idea behind this 7-day approach is to have something to look forward to. You mustn't stop exploring or trying new things, or else you will, once again, fall back into your old patterns of procrastinating and being content within your preconceived boundaries.

CREATING A VISION – DEALING WITH CHANGE

You need to keep moving forward and have something to work for—a goal, an interest, or simply an agenda that makes you wake up every morning excited and happy. This is where creating a vision comes in. Adapting to any type of change requires a willingness and an end goal. This end goal is the vision you aspire to reach. Change isn't easy. It doesn't motivate. But a vision, on the other hand, does. It gives you something to work toward. So how do you deal with change in a way that you remain motivated and aspire to keep moving forward and not waste your time or energy over unnecessary things?

Sit with what's uncomfortable. I have observed some motivational gurus asking their followers to ignore their problems, promising that they will go away on their own. Their aim is to prevent distraction and demotivation that comes from within us because we lose track of what we want and focus solely on what mishaps and challenges lay in the way. Some of you might find this advice works for you, but most of you won't.

I'll tell you why.

Doing so won't resolve your problems or the anxiety that comes with it. Instead, you will feel more and more anxious and unmotivated because you will start to view the challenge as something you can't overcome. You aren't an ostrich that ducks its head in the sand, thinking they become invisible. The challenges you face will catch up to you unless you address and acknowledge them.

The same is the case with change. You can't run away from it or turn a blind eye to it. You have to accept that it is happening and deal with it. Research shows that actively acknowledging negative emotions is the key to resolving them. In our case, this is how you will deal with any major changes in your life, like moving to a new school, starting a new job, getting into a relationship with someone, or moving out. Every emotion or challenge that comes with it will only be resolved if you sit with it, address that it's there, and find ways to make peace with it.

Stress a little, but not too much. This might come off as an unusual idea, but there has been research that suggests that stress can sometimes be a good thing as long as it is confined to some limits (Crum & Crum, 2015). Ever wondered why we stress? Ever noticed what stress tries to accomplish? A stressful situation is the time when you are your most creative. Isn't it true that when you are stressed about something, you think of a hundred ways to get out of it? Some of the ideas that your mind concocts are ones it wouldn't have concocted otherwise.

Stress might also be a sign that you are in a toxic environment and need to leave. Do you feel anxious before meeting a romantic partner because they can be extremely loud and suspicious of you? Maybe it is a sign that you need to end the relationship for the sake of your mental peace.

So stress is enough to get you through change without losing your mind.

Be flexible. Expecting stability isn't sensible when adapting to change. Things are going to be difficult at first—some practices you were used to will become obsolete. However, you can either be one of two people: You can choose to reminisce over the good ol' days and spend hours talking about how you were in control back then, and then someone or something came and took over that control, or you can choose to be someone who shows a willingness to adapt to their changing environment and cope with it. This can be an ideal situation for you to thrive in and learn more about yourself. Once you master the skill, you can, once again, take control.

The point is that you can't expect things to always be the same. People grow out of their habits, and we are talking about staying consistent. You need to adjust to what's going on and make that situation stable in your favor.

Identify problems. Finally, remember that while you take on a new path and turn the page over for a new chapter in your life, you are bound to come across some hardships. Challenges are how you learn something new. But is every problem an actual problem?

IS THIS A REAL PROBLEM?

For example, if you fail a test, maybe the reason isn't as simple as poor revision or lack of interest. Maybe it is stress about something else that prevented you from paying attention. It could also have been a distracted study environment or a lack of study material. This means that you might be solving the wrong problem when, in reality, it is something different. Sometimes, it is something else entirely that bothers you. So before you begin to panic, let's quickly learn how to identify a problem and how we can solve it.

A problem is any hardship or setback that prevents you from reaching your desired goal. Take, for instance, a lack of money to buy food. That's a problem. Your hunger can only be satisfied if you buy food from a store or restaurant. Until that issue is resolved, you will remain hungry, aka, in a state of misery.

But this is just a basic example with a solution as simple as borrowing money from a friend. What about bigger, more complex problems that don't show as clearly? There are ways to analyze them too.

Firstly, see if there is a deviation from set expectations. A problem is a sign of some form of deviation one expected.

Second, gather evidence that there is indeed a deviation. What evidence do you have? Did you fail or make a blunder? Did you fail to deliver what was expected? Did your habits change without you knowing?

Third, analyze the impact the problem creates. Is it preventing you from achieving your truest potential? Is it becoming a hurdle in your path?

Find out the root cause of it. What drives that problem? Now is the time to look for its causes. Is it as simple as it looks, or is it more complex than you think? Is it easy to overcome or difficult to solve?

Next, how are you going to solve it? Do you have the means and expertise to resolve it? Ideally, all you need to do is look at the causes and reverse them. It's like eliminating a bad habit. For instance, say you are using your phone too much. One major cause of this is boredom or loneliness. What you need is to use that cause and reverse it. In this case, you can find activities to keep yourself busy or hang out with your friends to keep your mind occupied.

This way, not only can you analyze a problem but also get to the root of it.

While you are at it, don't be fooled by the large chunks of information that you gather along the way. A problem can have several causes at once. Take your time to analyze each cause. Otherwise, you will only be touching the surface and not getting to its root.

Plan an integrated approach to cancel out most of the causes. Don't just work on one. Widen your focus and consider each cause.

Lastly, make sure to have a plan to avoid having the same problem repeated. It is only a sign that you weren't diligent enough the first time. And if it does occur again, you start the process again and hope for a more productive conclusion the next time.

AM I RIGHT TO PANIC?

Some major life changes, the ones you didn't think would be so sudden or traumatic can cause panic. For example, breaking up with someone or failing an important interview you prepared for keenly. They are going to appear as big setbacks that you didn't anticipate, or think would have such an effect on you. When starting a new school or job, most teenagers believe they have what it takes to handle the new circumstances. But in a few days or weeks, they realize, maybe not. They have trouble making friends, fitting in, or have a terrible boss who never appreciates their work.

If something of the sort happens, it is understandable to lose your footing and be stressed. But unless it is something that can't be solved, there isn't a need to panic. If the situation isn't dangerous or imminent, you can give yourself some time to reflect and then act. I believe as long as you are healthy and alive, you can always do something about your condition. I say this because I nearly lost my life during an accident a couple of years ago. I thought I would recover in no time with the help of my good friends and family.

But then COVID hit, and we all had to wait months before scheduling a trip to my maternal home, where my family lived. I felt hopeless because I couldn't move or go out. I felt isolated and lost. Every time my husband would go into the other room for a meeting, panic would set in. What if I needed to pee? What if a pigeon flew in from outside and sat on me? What if the house was on fire? Tons and tons of useless thoughts would creep up, leaving me stressed about nothing. I started asking my husband to attend his meetings from our room to calm myself. If that weren't possible, I would ask one of my kids to sit with me until Daddy returned. I just wanted to be watched.

It took me a while to come to terms with the aftermath of my accident. I had a neck brace in place and a dislocated leg joint that took months to heal. Once I was fully recovered and able to move, I realized there wasn't anything to worry about. I was just being overemotional. During therapy, my therapist helped me realize that my accident had little to do with my fear of being left alone and more with some childhood trauma. She helped me work through it and, thankfully, I was able to overcome the fear of being left alone.

In short, my accident wasn't the reason why I was panicking. It was because I never recovered from an earlier fear during my childhood. I realized as long as I was alive and willing to work through it, nothing could stop me. I knew panicking wasn't going to help me get better. It was only delaying the process of getting better. It was weakening me, putting all sorts of negative thoughts in my mind.

So if you ever feel overwhelmed by negative thoughts without reason and panic starts to set in, here are two strategies I learned in therapy to prevent it from becoming a meltdown:

5-4-3-2-1 Method

This is an excellent grounding technique that allows you to stay focused on the present and acclimate yourself to your current surroundings. You involve your five senses and try to divert your attention from something that's bothering you. To use this strategy, look for five things to see, four things to feel, three things to hear, two things to smell, and one thing to taste.

Doing so will help you calm your nerves and not let things overwhelm you.

3-3-3 Panic Alleviating Strategy

A similar strategy is the 3 3 3 strategy, where you look around yourself and find three objects, three moving body parts, and three sounds. For instance, if you are in class, look for three objects like the board, desks, and windows. For three moving body parts, you can notice your stomach, arms, and eyes. For three sounds, you can focus on the noise from the outside, birds, and the voice of your teacher or peers. The idea is to bring awareness to your present instead of getting triggered.

LIFE GETS HARD – NOW WHAT?

Acknowledging that there is a problem that needs solving is half the solution itself. It is the most important half, you could say. It sets the tone and determination for what you need to do. Since today's problems can become complex and challenging, they require more than just a simple breakdown. This is where problem prioritization comes in. Prioritizing your problems is all about finding the right ones to focus on and leaving the rest for another time. It's a lot like task prioritization, where you pick the most important or urgent one to work on first.

Problem prioritization promises the same. When you feel in control of your problems, you will feel less stressed about having them. One step at a time, as everyone says. But how do you prioritize a problem when all of them seem important and urgent?

You do it by using Eisenhower's Urgent-Important Matrix. Start with a box with four quadrants.

Quadrant 1: Urgent and important

These are the tasks that are top priority tasks. These can't be delayed or pushed back. They must be finished first thing.

Quadrant 2: Important but not urgent

These are high-value tasks minus a deadline, such as setting long-term goals, strategizing a vision for your future, or revising/improving on a college essay.

Quadrant 3: Urgent but not important

These tasks, although urgent in nature, don't require any special expertise. Things like setting reminders, delegating work, responding to work emails, making important calls, and so on all come under this third quadrant.

Quadrant 4: Not important nor urgent

Finally, some tasks eat up your focus and time despite being unimportant. Your goal should be to identify and eliminate those tasks so that you can have more time for the more important and urgent tasks. Here's a simple representation of how the matrix looks and how you can divide tasks based on their priority and urgency:

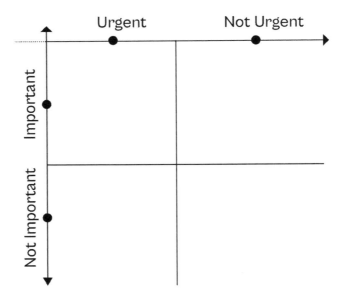

Once you are done prioritizing, learn how to problem-solve the most important ones.

Go back to doing root-cause analysis. There are several strategies you can use, but I want to talk about the three most effective and simple ones. Let's start with a basic one and then move on to more advanced ones.

12 What Elses

From the mind of author Lenedra J. Carroll, this technique allows you to come up with 12 answers for a particular problem (Valdellon, 2022). For instance, suppose you aren't able to land a part-time job while all your friends at school have one. This is a grave problem, especially when summer break is just around the corner, and you have nothing else to work for. Come up with 12 explanations as to what could be the reasons. For example, some of the reasons could be:

- not enough prior work experience.
- poor school grades.
- lack of references from teachers.
- a chaotic resume.
- inability to do well in interviews.
- poor time management.

Once you come up with 12 reasons, view each reason as another problem. For example, no prior experience becomes a new problem. Now establish 12 more explanations for this problem and keep going. As you go along, you will realize that some of the problems aren't as big as you thought they were. They are easy to resolve. For example, you can work on your time management skills by becoming more punctual and careful about where you spend your time. You could take a few classes or watch a few videos on how to do well in interviews. You can build a better resume online by using another template.

Once you have the means to resolve your problems, you can prioritize them based on their urgency. Building a CV is more important than working on your interview skills. You get the point, right?

Five Whys Root Cause Analysis

This is another fun and interesting way to prioritize problems. You start with a specific problem and then ask yourself five questions following it. Let me give you an example to show you how it works.

Problem: Not independent enough to move out.

Why?: It is because my parents do everything for me.

Why?: They see me as a sensitive child.

Why?: I was always fearful of people growing up.

Why?: I was once lost in the grocery store. It was a traumatic experience for me.

Why?: There were a lot of people, and they all looked the same.

Notice how one statement answers the reason for the previous one? That's how you get down to the root of a problem. You can also use the same method for different problems you face and prioritize them based on their severity and solution.

Hurson's Productive Thinking Model

Tim Hurson, a renowned author and guru, proposed a six-step model for problem-solving creatively (Mind Tools Content Team, n.d.).

You start by asking yourself, "**What is going on?**"

In the first step, you **define the problem and its impact**. Is having a weird roommate a problem, and is it preventing you from feeling safe within your apartment?

In the second step, you ask yourself, "**What is success?**"

This involves listing down what you must do, what you will need, the expected success rate of the solution you pick, and so on. Here, some solutions to consider are talking to your roommate, remaining distant and aloof, carrying pepper spray, or putting a lock on your room.

The third step is asking, "**What is the question?**"

This means you create a list of questions that will solve the problem when answered. For example, you can ask yourself what's preventing you from talking to your roommate, why you aren't putting a lock on your room, or buying pepper spray.

Generate answers in the fourth step.

Take questions from the third step and answer them.

The fifth step is to **forge a solution**.

Analyze each solution based on its expected success rate from step two. The one which seems most promising becomes the solution. You can, for instance, think about having an open conversation with your roommate and tell them why you feel uncomfortable around them and what they can do to make you feel more comfortable.

In the sixth and final step, **find resources to execute the solution**.

This is where you put into action the solution you came up with. You can have the conversation, and even if some problems don't get resolved or you think you messed up big time, remember that it isn't the end of the world. I keep telling teenagers how amazing and wholesome they are. They have their whole life ahead of them. They have their youth, their body doesn't ache, and they can be whoever they want to be.

So don't lose your heart or focus on something that isn't meant to be yours. Not every problem or circumstance is worth putting effort into. Sometimes, you have to leave things as they are and move on. Sometimes, you have to lose and accept that you lost and forget about it.

WHAT IF I MESSED UP?

Wait, what? But I thought the essay was good. How could I have gotten rejected?

I can't believe this happened. Are you sure it was my video of drinking last night that went viral? My parents are going to kill me.

But I thought those were the project requirements, sir. I thought I did my best. How can this not be selected?

Sometimes, things don't go as planned. Even our best efforts end in vain. We assume everyone thinks like us or likes the same thing as us. But people have different tastes and different opinions. What might seem tempting to you could be boring and uncreative to someone else. It is too easy to offend people these days. You can't be as expressive as you used to be because you have to think about everything you say or post online. Some consequences follow.

But let's not forget that we are human. We are free thinkers. We make mistakes. We are supposed to. Did you know that so many inventions would have never reached us had their inventors not made a boo-boo? Penicillin, potato chips, microwaves, Coca-Cola, and ice popsicles are just a few examples. Can you imagine living in a world without Coke?

Not every thought or idea we have results in success. Sometimes, things backfire, and it's okay as long as we don't think of it as the end of the world. So what if a video your friend posted online about pranking you goes viral? People are going to forget about it in a week or two. However, if you start thinking about how this will be the end of your life or career, you are in the wrong. No one today has the time to keep reliving the past. People move forward, and they move fast. This always means that they will forget about the messes you make along the way and focus on what's next.

But if you have your head stuck in the "I can't move forward from this. I will always be ridiculed. My career is forever gone . . ." you will stay in a pit without a ladder to climb out of it. So instead of wasting time praying for a time machine, here's what you can do.

Take accountability. You mess up, you own it. It's that simple. There is no need to be ashamed of it. Consider the biography of any celebrity, entrepreneur, or global magnate. They all made messes. They started small, failed, but kept going. That's what you are going to do.

Perhaps you hurt someone with your words, sent someone a shitty text, bullied a junior, or sabotaged a good friendship—take responsibility. There is no point blaming the circumstances or others for a mistake you made. When you take responsibility, you become more aware of the mistakes you made along the way. You become aware and cautious of them. You learn from the experience and grow. On the other hand, if you make yourself a victim, that's all you will ever be.

Next, you need to apologize, especially if your words or actions hurt someone's feelings. Apologize and be sincere about it. Accept that you were in the wrong and would like to be forgiven. Apologizing to someone is a sign of growth. It is very hard for some teenagers to admit to their mistakes—let alone apologize. Apologizing requires opening your heart, letting go of your ego, and accepting your faults. In short, it takes guts. How do you do it?

You begin by expressing regret. Then you explain what happened. You then take responsibility for the part you played in causing it and end with some strong suggestions on how you want to proceed to make someone feel better.

Don't be too harsh. It's easy to let the inner critic take over and delve into self-blame. Sure, you made a mistake. But that won't change who you are. You are still a young, competent teenager full of potential. Don't let one unwise decision demotivate you. Whenever I make a mistake, I ask myself what advice I would have given a friend who made the same mistake. Would I be harsh toward her? Would I offer unsolicited advice? Or would I show empathy and be there for her? Then I treat myself the same way I would treat a friend. I wouldn't be harsh or see myself as a failure in progress. I would see the mistake for what it is. I remind myself that I will not let the mistake define me. I will do better by being gentle and compassionate toward myself.

Stay present, and don't lose focus. It is easy to lose track of things when you are mourning your blunders. It is easy to just want to give up and visualize yourself living a dark future. Many children feel they will walk in the steps of an abusive or alcoholic parent the minute they default. They think that's who they are and will be in the future. This is rarely the case. You have a sane mind, you make your own decisions, and you have your dreams. How can someone mess with that unless you allow them to get into your head? Therefore, stop worrying about how this one failure will define your future. It won't. Focus on what you have. Focus on your strengths. Focus on your abilities and willingness to learn. Dwelling in the past won't bring any joy or hope. Doing so will keep you entangled in the what-ifs and worst-case scenarios. You won't be able to think straight or make better plans.

Start small. Make amends. Make sure that you learn from the experience and use it as a lesson to avoid making the same mess again. Forgive yourself and see it as an opportunity for growth instead of losing your heart. Set new expectations and devise plans to live up to those expectations.

That's how you grow and improve.

CHAPTER SUMMARY

5 Chapter Summary

Changing with the changing world is a prerequisite for adulthood. As you navigate teen ages, you learn something new every day. This chapter focuses on the **adaptation of change** as well as how to **problem-solve** the challenges that come along the way.

KEY TAKEAWAYS

5 Key Takeaways

1. **Change is inevitable**. The only way to keep up with the changing world is to have an open mind and attitude.
2. **Identify what problems are real problems**; know when to panic and how to resolve them by using the recommended techniques.
3. When you mess up, acknowledge your part in it, make amends, and move forward. **Don't remain stuck in a rut or label yourself as a failure**.

SUMMARY

 **Summary**

The Rolling Stones were right when they said time waits for no one.

For a teenager that is already going through enough, change isn't something that is easy. They have to find a new job, move out, get into a good college, and find their place in the world. This final chapter looks at how teenagers can adapt to their changing environment in a way that feels comfortable to them as well as learn how to solve their problems through resilience and grit. Some additional themes explored here include:

→ **How to identify problems.**

→ **Learning when it is okay** to panic and when it's not.

→ **Prioritizing problems** based on their importance and urgency using Eisenhower's Priority Matrix.

→ **Conducting a root-cause analysis** to get to the core of the problem and know if you are, indeed, solving the right problem or not.

→ **Learning how to own your messes** when you create them with humbleness and make up for them.

Leave Your Mark!

You're learning more about yourself and how to tackle the life ahead of you every day… and now you're feeling more confident, you're in a great position to help someone else embrace the same journey.

Simply by sharing your honest opinion of this book and a little about what you've discovered here, you'll help other teenagers find this essential guidance.

Thank you so much for your support. I'm excited about the journey ahead of you!

Scan the QR code to leave your review on Amazon.

(If you're feeling creative, snap a photo of your favorite chapter or a cozy reading nook and share it with your review).

CONCLUSION

 Learning is not attained by chance, it must be sought for with ardor and attended to with diligence.

— ABIGAIL ADAMS

There is so much to uncover, so much to practice, and so much to become acquainted with. Be it culture, people, or just the amazing scenery, there is always something new to look out for.

It's funny how they say that you never stop learning. From the moment you are born until the day you die, there is something new to explore and master. From ABCs to words and sentences, we learn.

Since human beings are curious by nature, it becomes an integral part of our growth. It only makes sense that you keep the tradition and curiosity alive as you enter this new phase of your life, full of opportunities and happiness.

Look at this as a chance to learn about anything and everything from anyone and everyone because that's how you are going to understand the purpose you were made for. That's how you are going to find out who you are as a person and a brand. You will know what you represent and bring to the table. It's important because we all are here to make a difference in someone's life. Whether we work under a boss or run an empire, we are a community designed for the welfare of people.

But before personal branding comes the task of knowing who you are. That, too, is only possible when we experience and try new things. We learn about our likes and dislikes through experiences—both good and bad. We realize a ton about our personalities, goals, and dreams. We understand that life isn't something to be wasted. It's precious and our only chance to make our mark. When you do, you start taking care of yourself. You eat better, drink more, and sleep well. You make time for your hobbies and interests and do what brings you joy. Most importantly, you delve deeper and take care of your mental and emotional state. You stop worrying about things out of your control and start looking forward to a better future.

This introspection allows us to learn about our habits, values, and purpose. With knowledge and exposure, we can better decide which habits and values benefit us, and which don't. This journey isn't a bed of roses either. You stumble, and you fall. You make mistakes and improvise. You accept responsibility and aim to do better.

Notice how it all comes down to the willingness to learn?

That's what this first book has been all about. Its vision was to put you, the teenager, the young blood, in the driver's seat, all armed to tackle bigger challenges. Now that you feel you are fully equipped with the knowledge you need to take care of yourself, your dreams, and your goals, the next journey will focus on what you need to learn and embrace to live the life of your dreams.

Remember how we talked about moving out, getting a job, and paying the bills? The next book in the series will focus solely on that and put all the knowledge you have gathered to use. It will be your test to prove how good you are or could be, provided that you put that knowledge to best use.

So are you ready to move forward with the same zest and zeal you had when you picked up this first book? Are you ready to challenge yourself? Are you ready to embrace the realities of living solo or in a shared space with a roommate?

Let's learn how to cook, clean, and manage money. Let's learn how to organize the house, stock the pantry, and redo the wardrobe. Together, let's learn how to do the laundry, use the dishwasher, and some basic etiquette.

Let's prove to your parents that you can look after yourself and make them proud. After all, you owe it to them and yourself.

Larissa Lawson

REFERENCES

Alfred A. Montapert quotes. (n.d.). BrainyQuote. https://www.brainyquote.com/quotes/alfred_a_montapert_109332.

Ayn Rand quotes. (n.d.). BrainyQuote. https://www.brainyquote.com/quotes/ayn_rand_124992.

Bard, E. (n.d.). *45 simple self-care practices for a healthy mind, body & soul.* Tiny Buddha. https://tinybuddha.com/blog/45-simple-self-care-practices-for-a-healthy-mind-body-and-soul/.

Bear Grylls quotes. (n.d.). BrainyQuote. https://www.brainyquote.com/quotes/bear_grylls_512988?src=t_survival.

Beck, C. (2022, April 5). *I messed up: What to do when you've made a mistake.* Supportiv. https://www.supportiv.com/tools/i-fucked-up-what-to-do-when-made-mistake.

Benna, S. (2015, August 6). *8 keystone habits that can transform your life.* Business Insider. https://www.businessinsider.com/keystone-habits-that-transform-your-life-2015-8.

Beresin, G. (n.d.). *11 self-care tips for teens and young adults.* MGH Clay Center for Young Healthy Minds. https://www.mghclaycenter.org/parenting-concerns/11-self-care-tips-for-teens-and-young-adults/.

Bernieri, F. J., & Petty, K. N. (2011). The influence of handshakes on first impression accuracy. *Social Influence, 6*(2), 78–87. https://doi.org/10.1080/15534510.2011.566706.

Betz, M. (2022, September 14). *What is self-awareness, and why is it important?* BetterUp. https://www.betterup.com/blog/what-is-self-awareness.

Bridges, F. (2019, February 25). *Five ways to make a habit stick.* Forbes. https://www.forbes.com/sites/francesbridges/2019/02/25/five-ways-to-make-a-habit-stick/?sh=6ec3b51c135b.

British Nutrition Foundation. (n.d.). *Hydration.* https://archive.nutrition.org.uk/healthyliving/hydration/adults-teens.html.

Chauncey, S. (2017, January 25). *Learning how to observe thoughts.* Living the Mess. https://www.livingthemess.com/learning-observe-thoughts/.

Cherry, K. (2023, April 137). *How to use a mood tracker.* Verywell Mind. https://www.verywellmind.com/what-is-a-mood-tracker-5119337.

Cherry, K. (2022, November 7). *What is self-concept?* Verywell Mind. https://www.verywellmind.com/what-is-self-concept-2795865.

Choi, H. K., & Curhan, G. (2008). Soft drinks, fructose consumption, and the risk of gout in men: Prospective cohort study. *BMJ, 336,* 309–312. https://doi.org/10.1136/bmj.39449.819271.be.

ChristineXP. (n.d.). *10 things every teen should know about dealing with a mental health issue.*

Discovery Mood & Anxiety Program. https://discoverymood.com/blog/10-tips-teen-dealing-with-a-mental-health/.

Clear, J. (2018). *How to start new habits that actually stick*. James Clear. https://jamesclear.com/three-steps-habit-change.

Crum, A., & Crum, T. (2015, September 3). *Stress can be a good thing if you know how to use it*. Harvard Business Review. https://hbr.org/2015/09/stress-can-be-a-good-thing-if-you-know-how-to-use-it.

Csikszentmihalyi, M. (1990). Flow: The psychology of optimal experience. Harper Perennial.

Dagfinn, A. (2012). Soft drinks, aspartame, and the risk of cancer and cardiovascular disease. *The American Journal of Clinical Nutrition, 96*(6), 1249–1251. https://doi.org/10.3945/ajcn.112.051417.

Dimberg, U., & Söderkvist, S. (2011). The voluntary facial action technique: A method to test the facial feedback hypothesis. *Journal of Nonverbal Behavior, 35*(1), 17–33. https://doi.org/10.1007/s10919-010-0098-6.

Ding, Q., Vaynman, S., Akhavan, M., Ying, Z., & Gomez-Pinilla, F. (2006). Insulin-like growth factor I interfaces with brain-derived neurotrophic factor-mediated synaptic plasticity to modulate aspects of exercise-induced cognitive function. *Neuroscience, 140*(3), 823–833. https://doi.org/10.1016/j.neuroscience.2006.02.084.

Duhigg, C. (2012). The power of habit: Why we do what we do in life and business. Random House.

Dutton, J. (2012, August 16). *Make your bed, change your life?* Psychology Today. https://www.psychologytoday.com/us/blog/brain-candy/201208/make-your-bed-change-your-life.

Emily Atack quotes. (n.d.). BrainyQuote. https://www.brainyquote.com/quotes/emily_atack_999785.

First impressions. (n.d.). Psychology Today. https://www.psychologytoday.com/us/basics/first-impressions.

Fletcher, C., & Bailey, C. (2003). Assessing self-awareness: Some issues and methods. *Journal of Managerial Psychology, 18*(5), 395–404. https://doi.org/10.1108/02683940310484008.

Gillihan, S. J. (2015, July 27). *Do you know what you need?* Psychology Today. https://www.psychologytoday.com/us/blog/think-act-be/201507/do-you-know-what-you-need.

Gonsenhauser, A. (2017, February 7). *Five easy steps to analyze any problem*. Forrester. https://www.forrester.com/blogs/fiveeasystepstoanalyzeanyproblem/.

Griffin, R. M. (n.d.). *11 natural depression treatments*. WebMD. https://www.webmd.com/depression/features/natural-treatments.

Hailey, L. (2022, April 15). How to set boundaries: 5 ways to draw the line politely. Science of People. https://www.scienceofpeople.com/how-to-set-boundaries/.

Handler, J. C. (2018, January 19). Identifying your feelings. Psychology Today. https://www.psychologytoday.com/us/blog/art-and-science/201801/identifying-your-feelings.

Harvard Health Publishing. (2019, May 1). *More evidence that exercise can boost mood..*

https://www.health.harvard.edu/mind-and-mood/more-evidence-that-exercise-can-boost-mood.

Heart & Stroke. (n.d.). *Healthy eating basics.* Heart and Stroke Foundation of Canada. https://www.heartandstroke.ca/healthy-living/healthy-eating/healthy-eating-basics.

Heitzman, A. (2022, May 19). *What is personal branding? Here's why it's so important.* Search Engine Journal. https://www.searchenginejournal.com/what-is-personal-branding-why-important/327367/#close.

Hodges, V. (n.d.). *Sense of self: What it is and how to build it.* Deepstash. https://deepstash.com/idea/183478/having-a-well-developed-sense-of-self-is-hugely-beneficial-in.

Hollis, J. F., Gullion, C. M., Stevens, V. J., Brantley, P. J., Appel, L. J., Ard, J. D., Champagne, C. M., Dalcin, A., Erlinger, T. P., Funk, K., Laferriere, D., Lin, P.-H., Loria, C. M., Samuel-Hodge, C., Vollmer, W. M., & Svetkey, L. P. (2008). Weight loss during the intensive intervention phase of the weight-loss maintenance trial. *American Journal of Preventive Medicine, 35*(2), 118–126. https://doi.org/10.1016/j.amepre.2008.04.013.

How to become more aware of your emotions and triggers with mood tracking. (2022, June 8). Ellie Mental Health. https://elliementalhealth.com/how-to-become-more-aware-of-your-emotions-and-triggers-with-mood-tracking/.

How to keep calm under pressure. (2017, November 14). Psychological Health Care. https://www.psychologicalhealthcare.com.au/blog/keep-calm-pressure/.

Identity crisis. (n.d.). Psychology. http://psychology.iresearchnet.com/social-psychology/self/identity-crisis/.

John Dryden quotes. (n.d.). BrainyQuote. https://www.brainyquote.com/quotes/john_dryden_101523.

Krasner, M. S., Epstein, R. M., & Beckham, H. (2009). Association of an educational program in mindful communication with burnout, empathy, and attitudes among primary care physicians. JAMA, 302(12), 1284. https://doi.org/10.1001/jama.2009.1384.

Lindberg, S. (2023, March 21). *22 ways to calm yourself down.* Healthline. https://www.healthline.com/health/how-to-calm-down.

Lloyd, S. L. (2022, December 5). *5 key ways to protect your heart in a relationship.* Brides. https://www.brides.com/protect-your-heart-4169324.

Loper, C. (2017, April 24). *Your chosen identity.* Northwest Educational Services. https://www.nwtutoring.com/2017/04/24/your-chosen-identity/.

Mann, C. R. (1918). *A study of engineering education* (pp. 106–107). The Carnegie Foundation For the Advancement of Teaching https://www.nationalsoftskills.org/downloads/Mann-1918-Study_of_Engineering_Educ.pdf.

Mark Twain quotes. (n.d.). Goodreads. https://www.goodreads.com/quotes/505050-the-two-most-important-days-in-your-life-are-the.

Mayureshwar, K., & Tarra, G. (n.d.). *First impressions are important, but shouldn't be defining.* El Estoque. https://elestoque.org/2021/11/04/uncategorized/first-impressions-are-important-but-shouldnt-be-defining/#:~:text=For%20teenagers%2C%20first%20impressions%20are.

Mental Health America. (n.d.-a). *Helpful vs harmful: Ways to manage emotions.* https://www.mhanational.org/helpful-vs-harmful-ways-manage-emotions.

Mental Health America. (n.d.-b). *The state of mental health in America.* https://mhanational.org/issues/state-mental-health-america.

Millar, K. (2020, January 21). *The importance of making a great first impression.* KM Transformational Branding Consultancy. https://www.kmtransformational.com/blog/the-importance-of-making-a-great-first-impression.

Mind Tools Content Team. (n.d.). *Hurson's productive thinking model.* Mind Tools https://www.mindtools.com/aqi5jjo/hursons-productive-thinking-model.

Mostafavi, B. (2018, September 17). *10 tips to help your teen sleep better.* Michigan Medicine. https://healthblog.uofmhealth.org/childrens-health/10-tips-to-help-your-teen-sleep-better.

National Institute of Mental Health. (2022, January). *Major depression.* U.S. Department of Health and Human Services. https://www.nimh.nih.gov/health/statistics/major-depression#part_155721.

Naumann, L. P., Vazire, S., Rentfrow, P. J., & Gosling, S. D. (2009). Personality judgments based on physical appearance. *Personality and Social Psychology Bulletin, 35*(12), 1661–1671. https://doi.org/10.1177/0146167209346309.

Nemours TeensHealth. (n.d.). *5 ways to help yourself through depression.* https://kidshealth.org/en/teens/depression-tips.html.

Pacheco, D. (2023, May 16). *Best temperature for sleep.* Sleep Foundation. https://www.sleepfoundation.org/bedroom-environment/best-temperature-for-sleep#:~:text=The%20best%20bedroom%20temperature%20for.

Pang, M. (2020, September 16). *How to ask for what you need.* Medium. https://betterhumans.pub/how-to-ask-for-what-you-need-583df84bee6e.

Paula. (n.d.). *9 self-care practices for the mind.* Thirteen Thoughts. https://www.thirteenthoughts.com/self-care-practices-for-the-mind/.

Personal values assessment. (n.d.). Personalvalu.es. https://personalvalu.es/.

Rauber, F., Steele, E. M., Louzada, M. L. da C., Millett, C., Monteiro, C. A., & Levy, R. B. (2020). Ultra-processed food consumption and indicators of obesity in the United Kingdom population (2008-2016). *PLoS ONE, 15*(5), 1–15. https://doi.org/10.1371/journal.pone.0232676.

Raypole, C. (2020, June 18). *'Who am I?' How to find your sense of self.* Healthline. https://www.healthline.com/health/sense-of-self.

Ridley, D. S., Schutz, P. A., Glanz, R. S., & Weinstein, C. E. (1992). Self-regulated learning: The interactive influence of metacognitive awareness and goal-setting. *The Journal of Experimental Education, 60*(4), 293–306. https://www.jstor.org/stable/20152338.

Risser, M. (2021, October 4). *11 ways to practice emotional self care.* Choosing Therapy. https://www.choosingtherapy.com/emotional-self-care/.

Robbins, T. (n.d.). *Develop your strengths.* Tony Robbins. https://www.tonyrobbins.com/stories/coaching/develop-your-strengths/.

Rowh, M. (2012, November). *First impressions count.* American Psychological Association. https://www.apa.org/gradpsych/2012/11/first-impressions.

Saweikis, S. (2020, May 5). *What to do when you really mess up and 9 steps to take.* Medium. https://sarahsaweikis.medium.com/what-to-do-when-you-really-mess-up-and-9-steps-to-take-505b0053d51o.

Schab, F. (2018, January 18). *The psychology of first impressions.* Six Degrees. https://www.six-degrees.com/the-psychology-of-first-impressions.

Schwartz, S. J., Hardy, S. A., Zamboanga, B. L., Meca, A., Waterman, A. S., Picariello, S., Luyckx, K., Crocetti, E., Kim, S. Y., Brittian, A. S., Roberts, S. E., Whitbourne, S. K., Ritchie, R. A., Brown, E. J., & Forthun, L. F. (2015). Identity in young adulthood: Links with mental health and risky behavior. *Journal of Applied Developmental Psychology, 36*, 39–52. https://doi.org/10.1016/j.appdev.2014.10.001.

ScienceBlog.com. (2002, October 27). *A smile really is contagious.* https://scienceblog.com/176/a-smile-really-is-contagious/.

7 reasons why you need to stay hydrated. (n.d.). Health for Teens. https://www.healthforteens.co.uk/lifestyle/8-reasons-why-you-need-to-stay-hydrated/.

Sidibé, A. (2022, January 30). Warren Buffett: The 5/25 rule. Medium. https://medium.com/@aliousidib/warren-buffet-the-5-25-rule-3d9093022f84.

Silvia, P. J., & O'Brien, M. E. (2004). Self-Awareness and constructive functioning: Revisiting "the human dilemma." *Journal of Social and Clinical Psychology, 23*(4), 475–489. https://doi.org/10.1521/jscp.23.4.475.40307.

Stephen Covey quotes. (n.d.). BrainyQuote. https://www.brainyquote.com/quotes/stephen_covey_138246.

Sutton, A., Williams, H. M., & Allinson, C. W. (2015). A longitudinal, mixed method evaluation of self-awareness training in the workplace. *European Journal of Training and Development, 39*(7), 610–627. https://doi.org/10.1108/ejtd-04-2015-0031.

Tartakovsky, M. (2015, August 7). *10 simple questions to help you identify or clarify your needs.* Psych Central. https://psychcentral.com/blog/weightless/2015/08/10-simple-questions-to-help-you-identify-or-clarify-your-needs#1.

Texas Exes. (2014, May 19). *University of Texas at Austin 2014 commencement address—Admiral William H. McRaven* [YouTube Video]. YouTube. https://www.youtube.com/watch?v=pxBQLFLei7o.

The Michael Page Team. (2023, February 2023). *Building your personal brand: Tips and strategies for crafting the brand called 'you.'* Michael Page. https://www.michaelpage.com.au/advice/career-advice/career-progression/personal-branding-how-build-brand-called-you-o.

Tila Tequila quotes. (n.d.). BrainyQuote. https://www.brainyquote.com/quotes/tila_tequila_510860.

"Top 100 Motivational Quotes (2023 Update)." Inspirational Quotes on Beautiful Wallpapers - QuoteFancy. Accessed October 23, 2023. https://quotefancy.com/motivational-quotes.

U.S. Department of Health and Human Services. (2018). *Physical activity guidelines for Americans 2nd edition.* https://health.gov/sites/default/files/2019-09/Physical_Activity_Guidelines_2nd_edition.pdf.

Valdellon, L. (2022, June 14). *Problem solving techniques and tips (that actually work).* Wrike. https://www.wrike.com/blog/problem-solving-techniques/.

Valentine, N. M. (1999). White House conference on mental health: Working for a healthier America. *Journal of the American Psychiatric Nurses Association, 5*(5), 167–171. https://doi.org/10.1177/107839039900500504.

Voigt, R. M., Forsyth, C. B., Green, S. J., Mutlu, E., Engen, P., Vitaterna, M. H., Turek, F. W., & Keshavarzian, A. (2014). Circadian disorganization alters intestinal microbiota. *PLoS ONE, 9*(5), e97500. https://doi.org/10.1371/journal.pone.0097500.

Wharton Executive Education, (2015, June 2). *Better decision-making: Identify the real problem.* https://executiveeducation.wharton.upenn.edu/thought-leadership/wharton-at-work/2015/06/identify-the-real-problem/.

What are the five whys? A tool for root cause analysis. (n.d.). Tulip. https://tulip.co/glossary/five-whys/#:~:text=Five%20whys%20(5%20whys)%20is.

Why is being self-aware important for your mental health? (2022, October 3). Alvarado Parkway Institute. https://apibhs.com/2022/10/03/why-is-being-self-aware-important-for-your-mental-health/.

Wooll, M. (2022, March 11). *How to get out of your comfort zone (in 6 simple steps).* BetterUp. https://www.betterup.com/blog/comfort-zone#%3A~%3Atext%3DThe%20best%20way%20to%20leave%2Clive%20a%20more%20fulfilling%20life.

Young, S. H. (2021, December 16). *18 tricks to make new habits stick.* LifeHack. https://www.lifehack.org/articles/featured/18-tricks-to-make-new-habits-stick.html.

Zaccaro, A., Piarulli, A., Laurino, M., Garbella, E., Menicucci, D., Neri, B., & Gemignani, A. (2018). How breath-control can change your life: A systematic review on psychophysiological correlates of slow breathing. *Frontiers in Human Neuroscience, 12.* https://doi.org/10.3389/fnhum.2018.00353.

Made in the USA
Middletown, DE
25 November 2024